Cambridge Student Guide

STRODE'S COLLEGE LIBRARY

Coriolanus

Gibson

Series Editor: Rex Gibson

CAMBRIDGE
UNIVERSITY PRESS

PUBLISHED BY THE PRESS SYNDICATE OF THE UNIVERSITY OF CAMBRIDGE
The Pitt Building, Trumpington Street, Cambridge, United Kingdom

CAMBRIDGE UNIVERSITY PRESS
The Edinburgh Building, Cambridge CB2 2RU, UK
40 West 20th Street, New York, NY 10011–4211, USA
477 Williamstown Road, Port Melbourne, VIC 3207, Australia
Ruiz de Alarcón 13, 28014 Madrid, Spain
Dock House, The Waterfront, Cape Town 8001, South Africa

http://www.cambridge.org

© Cambridge University Press 2004

This book is in copyright. Subject to statutory exception and to the provisions
of relevant collective licensing agreements, no reproduction of any part may
take place without the written permission of Cambridge University Press.

First published 2004

Printed in the United Kingdom at the University Press, Cambridge

Typeface 9.5/12pt Scala   *System* QuarkXPress®

A catalogue record for this book is available from the British Library

ISBN 0 521 53859 9 paperback

Cover image: © Getty Images/PhotoDisc

Contents

STRODE'S COLLEGE LIBRARY

Introduction

Coriolanus can be thought of as the story of a heroic soldier whose downfall is caused by pride and inflexibility of character. A different perspective views the play as an exploration of mother–son relationships: how Coriolanus' emotional attachment to his mother, Volumnia, both creates and destroys him.

But the play is more than the story of one man or his family relationships. It can be perceived as being structured into three phases: war, politics and betrayal. The play might then be interpreted as how war shapes Coriolanus, giving him success and identity; how politics bring him failure and banishment from Rome; and how his betrayal of Rome by his defection to the Volsces ends in his death.

Another approach to *Coriolanus* is to see it as a particular type of play. For example it has been identified as a tragedy in which a flaw in the hero's character causes his tragic fall, and as a history play about the early days of the Roman republic. A different reading views it as a kind of morality play: Shakespeare's dramatic adaptation of a story from the Roman historian, Plutarch, which Jacobeans read in order to learn lessons from the life of a particular individual.

Yet another perspective on the play is that it is Shakespeare's dramatisation of certain issues that preoccupied his contemporaries: the threat of civil disruption by an impoverished underclass protesting about enclosures and corn shortages, or the quarrels between King James I and Parliament over the right to make laws.

Many critics assert that *Coriolanus* is Shakespeare's most political play, a sustained exploration of the central question of government: who should hold power?

All the above are valid ways of thinking about the play. What makes it grippingly dramatic is the conflict that occurs at all levels: Romans versus Volsces, patricians versus plebeians, the personal animosity of Coriolanus and Aufidius, and family conflict as Volumnia makes her unwilling son plead for the citizens' votes. Within himself, Coriolanus experiences emotional conflict. He renounces his lifelong loyalty to Rome and then is doomed to destruction as his affection for his family overcomes his commitment to the Volsces' cause. Such personal and social conflict creates compelling theatre.

Commentary

Before the play begins

The story of *Coriolanus* is Shakespeare's version of events in the early days of the Roman republic, long before Rome became a great military empire. According to legend, Rome was founded in 753 BC by Romulus who, with his brother Remus, was supposed to have been suckled by a she-wolf. It was ruled by Etruscan kings, the Tarquins, until 509 BC when the last Tarquin king was driven out, and Rome became a republic.

Shakespeare's play is set around 490 BC, shortly after the republic was established. Rome was still a small city, just one of many in Italy where warring tribes fought each other. But it was a divided city. The patricians (aristocrats) and the plebeians (citizens) had united to drive out the Tarquins, but were now locked in a bitter struggle for power.

The patricians were the ruling class of Rome. They owned most of the property in the city, and wielded all the power. They alone held the right to become senators and make laws in the Senate. From their ranks came the Consuls, two of whom served for one year only with full executive powers as joint heads of the civil state and the army. Plebeians were the workers: servants, artisans, small traders and farmers, beggars. In the evolving republic, there was always smouldering resentment between the haves and the have-nots.

Republican Rome claimed that all the people had a part in affairs of state: making laws, declaring war, electing magistrates. But in practice the plebeians had little or no influence over political decisions, and they were economically exploited by the patrician class. Hard labour and military service were their daily conditions of life. Famine was an ever-present threat, just as it was for many of Shakespeare's contemporaries.

Act 1 Scene 1

The play explodes into action with the threat of a food riot. The citizens (plebeians) focus their anger on Caius Martius, the patrician warlord who later becomes known as Coriolanus. They resolve to rebel, and to kill Caius Martius because he and his fellow patricians have hoarded corn, causing the working people to starve. It is a spectacular opening moment as the stage fills with angry citizens brandishing weapons. To make clear the cause of potential revolt, the 1993 Royal Shakespeare Company production began with the citizens angrily watching a golden shower of corn fall into a pit on stage.

Shakespeare ensures that Caius Martius is always the subject of the drama, whether or not he is on stage, and the citizens' language immediately provides the first of many descriptions of his character that run through the play: 'chief enemy to the people', 'a very dog to the commonalty'. In what will become three of the major themes of the drama (pride, mother-love, valour) the First Citizen claims that Caius Martius seeks fame out of pride and a desire to please his mother. His pride is as great as his valour ('virtue'):

> Though soft-conscienced men can be content to say it was for his country, he did it to please his mother and to be partly proud, which he is, even to the altitude of his virtue.
>
> *(lines 28–30)*

The Second Citizen defends Coriolanus saying he is not greedy for wealth ('covetous'). But hearing shouts, the First Citizen assumes that other citizens are in active revolt and cries 'To th'Capitol!', probably intending to incite the citizens to storm the Senate. Menenius, a much-liked patrician, appears and attempts to calm the mob. His political skill is immediately evident as he uses flattering descriptions of the mutinous plebeians: 'my countrymen', 'mine honest neighbours', 'friends'. In a speech (lines 51–64) that is a mixture of soothing assurance and veiled threats, he claims that the patricians love the people, that the citizens are powerless against the Roman state, that the famine is caused by the gods, and that there is danger ahead ('transported by calamity' – made frantic by disaster). He ends by accusing the citizens of wrongly criticising the patricians ('The helms o'th'state' – helmsmen who steer the ship of state), who 'care for you like fathers'. In performance Menenius sometimes speaks in a kindly and friendly manner to ensure the plausibility of his argument. At other times, his manner is obviously patronising.

The Second Citizen denies Menenius' claim that the patricians care for Rome's ordinary people. Instead, they cause starvation by hoarding corn, support moneylenders ('usurers') who charge high rates of interest, and use the law to aid the rich and oppress the poor.

In response to the Second Citizen's list of injustices, Menenius proposes to tell a 'pretty tale' (apt story or fable). It is the tale of the belly, a parable which compares the stomach in the body to the patricians in the state. In performance, Menenius has used different story-telling styles, but often his mood is one of genial good humour, as if he were relating a fairy story to a group of children.

Menenius explains how the belly sends food to all parts of the body, and is left only with waste. He claims that the senators represent the belly, and the plebeians are the other body parts. His tale of the belly uses a comparison familiar to Shakespeare's audience: society as a human body. Such comparisons were intended to show that society is naturally hierarchical, with aristocrats deserving their elite status at the top. For Menenius the belly is the patrician class, the source of all 'public benefit' in the state. In short, it is a claim that rich rulers serve the poor and get nothing for their pains.

Menenius' tale illustrates a familiar trick of politicians in all ages. They know that style (how something is said) is just as important as substance (what is said). In Shakespeare's time, as in ancient Rome, public speakers learned the rules of rhetoric (the art of speaking well, so as to persuade the hearers). The plebeians listening to Menenius' fable of the belly are angry that the patricians are hoarding corn. But Menenius intends his tale to defuse the riot.

One quality of successful story-telling is how the narrator uses all kinds of delaying devices (pauses, distractions, added detail, etc.) to stretch out the tale and make the listeners keen to hear more. Menenius' tale allows the actor to exploit all these devices. For example, the actor often belches at 'even thus' (line 91), and he uses humour when he calls the Second Citizen 'the great toe of this assembly' to deflect attention from the truth of his story. But Menenius' apparently friendly tone towards the plebeians suddenly changes (he has perhaps seen Caius Martius approaching). He now directly insults them as 'rats' (line 145) who will soon be at war with Rome (the patricians). That change of mood is vividly underlined by Caius Martius' first words as he contemptuously addresses the citizens:

> What's the matter, you dissentious rogues,
> That, rubbing the poor itch of your opinion,
> Make yourselves scabs? *(lines 147–9)*

This is the audience's first sight of Caius Martius, and Shakespeare immediately establishes his character as he delivers a stream of invective against the plebeians, accusing them of cowardice and inconsistency. Shakespeare found the story of Coriolanus in the writings of the Roman historian, Plutarch (see page 75). There, he read that Caius Martius 'was so choleric [full of anger] and impatient that he would yield to no living creature, which made him churlish, uncivil, and altogether unfit for any man's conversation'. Shakespeare provides Martius with language to match Plutarch's description, giving him a tirade of scornful abuse against the plebeians. It is full of antitheses (opposing words or phrases, see page 89) to emphasise their cowardice and fickleness:

> What would you have, you curs,
> That like nor peace nor war? The one affrights you,
> The other makes you proud. He that trusts to you,
> Where he should find you lions finds you hares,
> Where foxes, geese you are – no surer, no,
> Than is the coal of fire upon the ice,
> Or hailstone in the sun. *(lines 151–7)*

Hearing that the citizens want corn, Martius continues his contemptuous diatribe. He is disgusted that the plebeians dare to discuss affairs of state, and wishes that he could kill them all ('I'd make a quarry / With thousands of these quartered slaves' (lines 181–2), 'quarry' – a heap of slaughtered deer). He ridicules the proverbs used by the plebeians as childish slogans. Martius is outraged that the plebeians have been granted tribunes (spokesmen and defenders of their rights) and predicts that civil strife will result. He thinks the concession will kill off the nobility ('break the heart of generosity') because it is a step towards democracy. He would rather see Rome destroyed than grant any influence to the people, and sees trouble ahead as the plebeians undermine the patricians' power:

> 'Sdeath,
> The rabble should have first unroofed the city
> Ere so prevailed with me! It will in time
> Win upon power and throw forth greater themes
> For insurrection's arguing. *(lines 200–4)*

A messenger brings news that the Volsces are preparing for battle. The news delights Martius who sees war as a way 'to vent / Our musty superfluity'. The literal meaning is 'we will have ways of getting rid of the surplus of our old rotten corn'. Martius is thinking of the rebellious citizens of Rome, and expressing the belief that war is like a medicine that cleanses society, killing off the excess population. The image echoes a popular medical practice in Shakespeare's time: blood-letting. Doctors drained blood from a sick person, believing that an excess of blood caused the illness. Martius thinks the blood of the plebeians must be shed to purge the Roman state.

Martius praises the Volsces' leader, Aufidius, and looks forward to fighting him. He is appointed second-in-command to Cominius, and with a final sneer at the citizens' cowardice (like rats they can eat the Volsces' corn store), he departs for the war. The stage clears as the 'Citizens steal away' (in many productions clearly fearful of the coming war), and, as will happen at the end of other scenes, the two tribunes are left to comment on the action. They remark on Martius' excessive pride, and say that whether Cominius succeeds or fails, the result will improve Martius' reputation and honour. They decide to watch the preparations for war ('dispatch') and whether Martius shows anything other than his usual pride ('singularity'):

> Let's hence, and hear
> How the dispatch is made and in what fashion,
> More than his singularity, he goes
> Upon this present action.   *(lines 260–3)*

Act 1 Scene 2

Throughout the play Shakespeare's dramatic construction will ensure striking contrasts. The previous scene has established the opposition of the patricians and plebeians of Rome. Now, as the location shifts to the city of Corioles, Shakespeare shows the Volsces, bitter enemies of Rome. Some productions ensure the contrast is visually emphatic, portraying the Volsces quite different in appearance from the Romans. The 1972 Royal Shakespeare Company production showed them like Aztec warriors, dressed in elaborate feathered costumes, who held their meeting, like a religious ritual, around a blazing fire.

The scene reveals that both Romans and Volsces have spies,

reporting on their opponents' military preparations. Aufidius reads the letter from his own spy which tells of a famine in Rome provoking the citizens to mutiny. But the letter also reports that the Roman army is most likely advancing on the city of Corioles. Aufidius is appointed general of the Volscian army ('Take your commission'), sometimes staged as an elaborate ceremony.

Scene 2 makes clear the political and military antagonism of the Volsces and the Romans, and the personal rivalry of Aufidius and Martius. Aufidius vows to fight his arch rival to the death:

> If we and Caius Martius chance to meet,
> 'Tis sworn between us we shall ever strike
> Till one can do no more. *(lines 34–6)*

Act 1 Scene 3

In contrast to the exclusively male atmosphere of Scenes 1 and 2, so much concerned with conflict, Scene 3 presents the women of the play in a domestic setting. Coriolanus' mother and wife sit, sewing. As they talk, their contrasting characters are established. Volumnia wishes Virgilia were more cheerful, and tells how happily she sent Martius to battle when he was very young, 'To a cruel war I sent him'. It is clear that Volumnia values 'honour', 'war', and being 'a man' over being a loving husband to Virgilia. She takes pleasure in Martius having returned from his first battle with 'his brows bound with oak' (encircled with oak leaves, the reward for saving a Roman's life in battle).

Virgilia asks how Volumnia would have felt if Martius had died in battle. Her question prompts Volumnia's retort that she would prefer to have eleven sons killed in warfare than for one to live in sensual luxury. She goes on to imagine Martius killing Volsces and conquering Aufidius, and her language provides many clues to what she and her son are like. She tells of his joy in bravery in battle, his contempt for plebeian soldiers, and his glory in destruction and death (the image is of a harvestman who must mow an entire field or lose his wages):

>   His bloody brow
> With his mailed hand then wiping, forth he goes,
> Like to a harvestman that's tasked to mow
> Or all or lose his hire.   *(lines 29–32)*

Virgilia is shocked ('O Jupiter, no blood!'), but Volumnia is contemptuous of her fear and claims that pride in wounds received in battle are the sign of manhood. In a chilling image from Greek mythology, she tells of Hecuba, Queen of Troy, whose son, Hector, was killed in the siege of Troy:

>   The breasts of Hecuba,
> When she did suckle Hector, looked not lovelier
> Than Hector's forehead when it spit forth blood
> At Grecian sword, contemning.   *(lines 35–8)*

Valeria enters and asks after Virgilia's son. Volumnia and Valeria reveal that young Martius shares his father's liking for war and destruction. Valeria's tale of how young Martius savagely destroyed a butterfly confirms her claim that the boy is indeed 'the father's son', a chip off the old block.

In many productions Valeria is played as a light-hearted gossip who uses the affected speech style of a fashionable lady, for example in her repeated use of 'la'. Later in the play you will discover that Coriolanus describes her very differently (see page 63). Virgilia refuses all her entreaties to go visiting. She has sworn not to leave the house until Martius returns. Her refusal prompts Valeria to describe her as 'another Penelope'. The image is again from Greek mythology. Penelope was the faithful wife of Ulysses. He left his home in Ithaca for the Trojan wars. During his absence, she refused to marry any of her many suitors ('moths' – parasites) until she had finished weaving a shroud. Each night she unpicked her weaving to ensure that she would never finish. Her name became the symbol of the faithful wife, and Shakespeare probably uses it here to suggest Virgilia's character.

Valeria has news of Martius. He is besieging Corioles and expects an early victory. Virgilia resists another invitation to leave the house. The scene has clearly established the difference between her and her fiery mother-in-law, Volumnia.

Act 1 Scene 4

Scenes 4–10 portray the war between Rome and the Volsces. As Valeria reported at the end of Scene 3, the Romans have divided into two armies. One, under Cominius, fights the Volsces at a place about a mile and a half from Corioles (line 9). The other Roman army, commanded by Martius and Lartius, is on stage, facing the walls of the city of Corioles. The scene opens with Martius and Lartius light-heartedly betting on whether Cominius has fought with the Volsces.

Martius prays to Mars, the Roman god of war, for quick success in the battle. The Volscian Senator appears on the walls of the besieged city and defies and taunts Martius and the Romans. Martius orders an advance, but the Volsces drive the Romans back ('alarums' are trumpet calls or the noise of battles and skirmishes). You can find accounts on pages 13 and 105–6 of how the battle was staged in the nineteenth and twentieth centuries, and every modern production tries to make the action as thrilling as possible. Sometimes the fighting is acted realistically, at other times symbolically, in slow motion, with tableaux (frozen stage pictures).

Martius displays unflagging bravery, and is enraged by what he sees as his soldiers' cowardice. He wants to rally his retreating soldiers, and to motivate them to attack the Volsces once more, but can only find language to curse them:

> All the contagion of the south light on you,
> You shames of Rome! You herd of – boils and plagues
> Plaster you o're, that you may be abhorred
> Farther than seen, and one infect another
> Against the wind a mile! You souls of geese
> That bear the shapes of men, how have you run
> From slaves that apes would beat!
>
> . . .
>
>   Come on!
> If you'll stand fast, we'll beat them to their wives,
> As they us to our trenches. Follow!
>
> *(lines 31–7 and 41–3)*

But his soldiers refuse to follow, and Martius enters Corioles alone and is shut in as the gates close behind him. The soldiers comment sardonically on his fate, thinking he will be killed because he is now trapped inside the city. 'To th'pot, I warrant him' means 'to the cooking pot' (he's in the soup, his goose is cooked). Titus Lartius enters and, being told what has happened, praises Martius' bravery, comparing him to a perfect jewel ('carbuncle entire') and a soldier whom Cato would have admired (Cato was a historian who acclaimed traditional Roman virtues).

At that moment Martius emerges from the city gates, wounded but still fighting. Martius' reappearance, apparently from the dead, makes an intensely exciting moment of theatre and is usually staged with great spectacle. In one production he appeared drenched from head to foot in blood. In another, he appeared at the top of the walls, forcing apart the huge gates of the city. In a modern dress production, he clung to the hook of a giant crane which lifted him over the walls. He fired his rifle at the Volsces and threw grenades, blasting a breach in the city walls through which the Roman army charged. He has single-handedly turned the tide of battle, and the Roman soldiers follow him into Corioles to capture the city.

Act 1 Scene 5

Shakespeare again writes a contrasting scene. After Martius' heroics in Scene 4, Scene 5 opens with Roman soldiers emerging from Corioles carrying off their loot. Martius is contemptuous of the looters, saying they steal worthless things. Shakespeare makes the contrast very obvious between Martius' concern only with victory and honour, and the soldiers' with carrying off whatever booty they can find.

Martius orders Lartius to guard the city whilst he goes to help Cominius. He claims that fighting has refreshed, not tired him, and leaves to join Cominius' battle, and hoping to fight personally with Aufidius.

Act 1 Scene 6

Scene 5 ends with Martius leaving Corioles. Scene 6 opens at a place just over one mile away, where Cominius and his troops are taking a brief rest in their fiercely fought battle. Cominius rallies his men and prays for the success of both Roman armies. His leadership style as he attempts to motivate his men noticeably contrasts with how Martius had tried to rally his own troops in Scene 4:

Breathe you, my friends. Well fought! We are come off
Like Romans, neither foolish in our stands,
Nor cowardly in retire.

. . .

The Roman gods
Lead their successes as we wish our own,
That both our powers, with smiling fronts encountering,
May give you thankful sacrifice!

(lines 1–3 and 6–9)

A messenger brings news of the earlier Roman retreat at Corioles.
Cominius is suspicious, asking why he took so long to cover a fairly
short distance from Corioles. Messengers in Shakespeare's plays
often get badly treated. In one production, Cominius was about to
strike the Messenger, but stopped as Martius appeared, drenched in
blood. Cominius at first does not recognise him, and says that he
looks as if he has been skinned alive ('flayed').

Martius embraces Cominius, saying he feels the same emotions he
felt on his wedding night. Much later (see page 50) Aufidius will use
the same sexual image when greeting Coriolanus; perhaps it suggests
the erotic bonding which the male warriors in the play experience for
each other. He tells how Titus Lartius is imposing military law on
Corioles, and uses an unflattering image for the captured city,
comparing it to a 'fawning greyhound' (flattering dog). But he vents
his wrath on the common soldiers again, using an even more
contemptuous image to describe their cowardice:

But for our gentlemen,
The common file – a plague! Tribunes for them! –
The mouse ne'er shunned the cat as they did budge
From rascals worse than they.   *(lines 42–5)*

Martius bombards Cominius with questions on his battle. It hardly
sounds like a second-in-command speaking to his commanding
officer, but the tone and style are typical of Martius. He then implores
Cominius to let him fight Aufidius. Cominius agrees and invites him
to choose the soldiers to accompany him against Aufidius. Martius'
call for volunteers is very different from the abusive language he used
against his retreating troops in Scene 4:

If any such be here,
As it were sin to doubt, that love this painting
Wherein you see me smeared; if any fear
Lesser his person than an ill report;
If any think brave death outweighs bad life,
And that his country's dearer than himself,
Let him alone, or so many so minded,
Wave thus [*Waving his sword*] . . .   (lines 67–74)

The appeal to their courage is entirely successful, and Shakespeare's stage direction vividly expresses the soldiers' response:

> *They all shout and wave their swords, take him up in their arms,*
> *and cast up their caps*   (following *line 75*)

Martius seems overwhelmed. After all his reviling of the common people, he has succeeded in winning their support, 'O'me alone! Make you a sword of me?' (line 76). He praises the soldiers and resolves to select the numbers he needs.

Act 1 Scenes 7 and 8

In the very brief Scene 7 Titus Lartius gives orders for Corioles to be guarded and leaves to support Cominius in the coming battle. In Scene 8 Martius and Aufidius at last meet face to face, and exchange insults. Aufidius' taunt, comparing Martius with Hector, is based on Greek legend. The Trojan hero, Hector, was the 'whip' (scourge, punisher) of the Greeks who besieged Troy. One of the besieging Greeks was Aeneas, the legendary founder of Rome, and therefore one of the ancestors of whom Martius may have boasted ('your bragged progeny').

Martius boasts of his single-handed victory in Corioles, and he and Aufidius fight. Martius gets the better of Aufidius. In dramatic contrast to Martius' victory at Corioles ('Alone I fought'), Aufidius needs other soldiers to help him survive, but resents his rescue by the Volsce soldiers ('condemnèd seconds' – damnable support):

> Officious and not valiant, you have shamed me
> In your condemnèd seconds.   (lines 14–15)

Act 1 Scene 9

The opening stage direction shows that the battle is over. After some sounds of fighting ('Alarum'), a trumpet call orders the pursuit of the fleeing enemy to be ended ('retreat'). Another trumpet call ('Flourish') announces victory. Martius appears with his arm in a sling. Cominius begins a speech in praise of Martius, promising to report his brave deeds in Rome where they will evoke admiration in the hearts of all who listen. Even the tribunes will thank the gods that Rome has such a soldier as Martius. But Martius wants no praise, and acknowledges that other soldiers have played their part. His words reveal a modesty and generosity not seen before, and show how much his mother and Rome are constantly in his thoughts (lines 13–19).

Cominius, however, insists that Martius' heroic actions must be proclaimed, and proposes to speak of them to the army. Martius continues to protest, saying his wounds will 'smart / To hear themselves remembered' (lines 28–9). Cominius' response to Martius' claim that his wounds would ache to hear praise often presents difficulties of understanding for a modern audience, but a probable paraphrase is 'If your wounds did not ache, they would become corrupt ('fester') in the face of lack of public gratitude, and cure themselves with death' (a 'tent' was a bandage used to keep wounds clean).

Martius refuses the offer of taking one tenth of the captured booty before it is shared between soldiers of the army ('common distribution'). The soldiers cheer his decision, shouting his name and throwing their caps and lances in the air. Cominius and Lartius remove their helmets as a mark of great respect. But Martius rounds on the soldiers passionately, calling for silence. He hates to hear the instruments of war (the long flourish of drums and trumpets) used for flattery, or swords ('steel') put to use other than killing. When that happens, he says, all civilian life will be hypocritical flattery ('false-faced soothing'), and a flatterer ('parasite') will become like 'An ovator': someone fit to lead an army and to receive public praise.

Martius plays down his own achievements ('my little') as a mere nosebleed or defeat of a feeble opponent ('foiled some debile wretch'). Many others have done the same without it being recorded ('without note'). He rejects such over-the-top praise ('acclamations hyperbolical'). But Cominius will not be denied, and calling Martius

'Too modest' praises him again, gives him his horse, and awards him the title by which he will henceforth be known, Coriolanus.

It is a spectacular moment of acclamation and honour, usually staged with great ceremony. But Coriolanus' response is downbeat in the extreme, 'I will go wash' (line 67), a line that often evokes audience laughter. However, he thanks Cominius and promises to live up to his new title, vowing to do justice to his new name to the utmost of his power ('undercrest your good addition . . . power' (lines 71–2)). An undercrest was a motto at the base of a coat of arms. He requests that a captured Volscian, who was once his kind host, be set free. But Coriolanus cannot remember the man's name, a failure of memory that some critics interpret as another clue to his character: an inability to see others as fully human.

Act 1 Scene 10

In Scene 9 Martius took on a new name as Coriolanus. In contrast, in Scene 10, Aufidius regrets that in defeat, and feeling disgrace at the capture of Corioles, he has lost his Volsce identity ('I cannot . . . be that I am'). In his anger and desire for revenge, he swears by earth, air, fire and water ('By th'elements') to end the personal rivalry by the death of himself or Coriolanus. He abandons chivalry, and swears nothing will protect Coriolanus against his revenge. He determines to beat Coriolanus using any form of trickery. Utterly determined, Aufidius lists eight examples of 'privilege and custom' that he vows will not protect Coriolanus from his hate:

> Nor sleep nor sanctuary,
> Being naked, sick, nor fane nor Capitol,
> The prayers of priests, nor times of sacrifice   *(lines 19–21)*

Not one of those 'Embarquements (restraints) all of fury' shall guard Coriolanus against Aufidius' hate. Aufidius resolves that he will adjust to circumstances ('the pace' of 'the world') in order to achieve what he wants. As the play unfolds, it becomes clear this is precisely what Coriolanus refuses to do: unlike Aufidius, he cannot and will not be flexible.

Act 1: Critical review

Act 1 establishes the conflicts that will create strife throughout the play. There is factional antagonism between patricians and plebeians; Romans are pitted against Volsces in war. Coriolanus and Aufidius are locked in bitter personal rivalry. In face-to-face combat Coriolanus proves the superior warrior, but Aufidius menacingly vows to use any treacherous means to overcome his rival.

Coriolanus begins the act as Caius Martius, but his awesome bravery at Corioles results in him being awarded the name that gives the play its title. But although his name may change, Coriolanus' character remains implacably constant. He despises the plebeians, and the contempt he shows them in his very first words will be confirmed as the play unfolds. He reviles them as cowards before Corioles, but in Scene 6 untypically feels brief solidarity with them as they acclaim him: 'O'me alone! Make you a sword of me?' (line 76).

Scene 3 reveals Volumnia has moulded her son into a terrifying fighting machine. She rejoices in warfare, and in an unnerving image, declares she finds a son's bloody wounds more lovely than mother's milk. Her idea of manhood as winning honour on the battlefield strikingly contrasts with Virgilia's fear. Mother and wife represent opposing attitudes to the military values of Rome.

Although Act 1 is primarily concerned with warfare, Menenius' fable of the belly in the opening scene introduces the political dimension that will characterise much of the play. The fable, a favourite of King James I, with its picture of an elite class serving the state selflessly without reward, is patently false. Nonetheless it represents the patrician ideology that underpins Coriolanus' belief in his personal and social superiority to the plebeians.

Act 1 shows Shakespeare creating the contrasts that are an integral element of his dramatic construction. Scene contrasts with scene as the action switches from Rome to Antium, and from public affairs to the domesticity of mother and wife sewing together at home. On the battlefield, Coriolanus' arrogant and sneering leadership is set against Cominius' positive motivation of his troops, and Coriolanus' valour is opposed to the plebeian soldiers' reluctance to fight and concern for loot.

Act 2 Scene 1

The action shifts back to Rome, and the factional conflict between patricians and plebeians shown in Act 1 Scene 1 is again made evident as the patrician Menenius mocks the tribunes, the representatives of the citizens. As they try to gain the advantage of each other in word-play, much of their talk is about Coriolanus' pride. All three men still speak of him as Martius, because news has not yet reached Rome of his victory at Corioles.

The political opponents verbally fence together, and on four occasions the tribunes speak together, reinforcing the sense of their solidarity and shared values. Menenius defends Coriolanus, accuses the tribunes of impatience, and promises to tell them what the patricians think of them ('us o'th'right-hand file' means 'we patricians, right wingers': in battle the best troops fought in the right-hand file). Menenius continually tries to score off the tribunes, and they try to get the better of him, and to deflect his humour. In performance the joking has sometimes been played as light-hearted, but there is no doubt that a profoundly serious enmity lies behind the exchanges, strongly hinted at in the imagery of the wolf, lamb and bear. Early in the exchange Menenius call the tribunes 'old men', which may be a joke or an insult, even if it is an accurate description. But Menenius then directly insults them:

> a brace of unmeriting, proud, violent, testy magistrates,
> alias fools   *(lines 35–6)*

In the following great flow of language (lines 38–75) Menenius whimsically lists his own failings, then describes the tribunes' inept performance as magistrates. Menenius sometimes speaks his tirade very fast, making it difficult for the audience to make sense of every word. That may be his intention, because he wants to make the tribunes feel inferior, and confuses them by making up phrases like 'bisson conspectuities' (line 51), which means 'bleary-eyed sight'. It is helpful to summarise what Menenius says as he first describes himself, then launches into his mockery of the tribunes (echoing criticism of magistrates in Shakespeare's London).

Lines 38–52. I like my liquor undiluted ('allaying Tiber' – diluting water, the River Tiber flows through Rome), I judge in favour of the first speaker in a case, and am quick-tempered about trivial matters. I love late-night parties and say the first thing that comes into my head. You two are common politicians (unlike Lycurgus, a famous Greek lawyer) who give me bellyache. You mainly speak like donkeys, and people lie who say you are honest. What faults can your blurred vision find in me?

Lines 54–65. You are totally ignorant, wanting people to bow and scrape to you. You spend a very long time judging a trivial case, and all your face-pulling and shouting make it even more muddled, and you simply blame both parties in the case. Here Brutus manages to get a word in, saying Menenius is better known as a joker ('giber') than an important judge ('necessary bencher').

Lines 66–75. You are a laughing-stock, who talk nonsense and are without honour. Martius is better than all your ancestors put together ('Deucalion' was the equivalent of Noah in Greek myth). Menenius ends with a final dismissive insult comparing the tribunes to mere shepherds of stupid sheep:

> More of your conversation would infect my brain, being the
> herdsmen of the beastly plebeians.   *(lines 74–5)*

Menenius' language undergoes a sudden change when the three Roman ladies enter. His mocking of the tribunes changes to courteous greeting ('as fair as noble ladies'), emphasising the social distance between the plebeians and the patricians. Talking with the ladies, and learning that Coriolanus will shortly arrive and has sent him a letter, Menenius continues to display his pleasure in showing off his knowledge and his delight in witty images. He says the letter is better than any medicine: Galen was a famous Greek doctor, and 'empericutic' (line 91) and 'fidiussed' (line 104) are made-up words. They probably mean 'false medicine' and 'Aufidiussed' (a pun on Aufidius' name, implying 'thrashed'). He rejoices at news that Coriolanus is returning to Rome, wounded but wearing around his brows a victory wreath of oak leaves ('the oaken garland' – line 99). The responses of friend, mother and wife to Coriolanus' wounds reveals much about their characters:

MENENIUS Is he not wounded? He was wont to come home
    wounded.
VIRGILIA O no, no, no!

VOLUMNIA O, he is wounded; I thank the gods for't.
MENENIUS So do I too, if it be not too much.   *(lines 92–6)*

Volumnia and Menenius rejoice in Coriolanus' military achievements, and vie with each other in counting his wounds. In previous battles he had sustained twenty-five wounds; now, says Menenius ecstatically, 'it's twenty-seven. Every gash was an enemy's grave' (line 125). Hearing the sound of trumpets, Volumnia chillingly celebrates her son's death-dealing power:

> These are the ushers of Martius. Before him
> He carries noise, and behind him he leaves tears.
> Death, that dark spirit, in's nervy arm doth lie,
> Which being advanced, declines, and then men die.
>
> *(lines 127–30)*

What follows is usually staged spectacularly, as Coriolanus makes his triumphal entry, and is greeted with the repeated shout from all: 'Welcome to Rome, renownèd Coriolanus!' (line 136). He had gone to battle under the command of Cominius, but returns as the chief hero of the war. But true to character, Coriolanus rejects praise and disdains adulation: 'No more of this, it does offend my heart.' He kneels to his mother, and some productions try to evoke audience laughter by suggesting that Volumnia has an unexpected sense of humour. For example, she smiles and shows she is unsure how to pronounce her son's new name. 'What is it?' she asks, experimenting amusedly with 'Cor-ee-olanus' and 'Cor-eye-olanus'. Shakespeare significantly keeps Virgilia silent but has her weep. Coriolanus greets her as 'My gracious silence' and tells her that she looks as sad as the widows of the men he has slain.

Menenius welcomes Coriolanus and again insults the tribunes, this time as 'old crabtrees' (line 158) who refuse to welcome the hero. Coriolanus now seems to touch his mother and wife, 'Your hand, and yours' (but in some productions this line is addressed to Menenius and Cominius), and intends to report to the patricians. His words prompt Volumnia's political ambitions for her son: she hopes Coriolanus will become Consul (one of the two most powerful political officials in Rome). It is the 'one thing wanting' that will fulfil her wishes and imaginings ('inherited . . . buildings of my fancy'.)

Coriolanus responds to his mother's words by expressing his contempt for the plebeians: he would rather be their servant and retain his true nature ('my way') than rule over ('sway with') them and change his nature. His inflexibility predicts the conflicts that lie ahead, and Shakespeare makes that dramatically obvious as the triumphal procession moves on, leaving the stage empty, but for the two tribunes. Their animosity and fears are evident as Brutus describes how everybody wished to see Coriolanus' entry into Rome. His words paint a vivid picture of the welcome the patrician hero received from neglectful nurses, kitchen maids and all kinds of people ('variable complexions') as they climbed on sales counters and roofs to see him. Even rarely seen priests ('Seld-shown flamens') joined in the adulation, and high-born ladies threw off their veils, risking suntans (which were unfashionable in Shakespeare's time) to greet Coriolanus.

The tribunes fear they will lose power if Coriolanus is made Consul, but predict that his anger and pride will cause his downfall. They see their opportunity to bring him down in his refusal to appear humbly before the people at election time:

> I heard him swear,
> Were he to stand for consul, never would he
> Appear i'th'market-place nor on him put
> The napless vesture of humility,
> Nor showing, as the manner is, his wounds
> To th'people, beg their stinking breaths.   *(lines 202–7)*

The tribunes plan to inflame the plebeians' anger against Coriolanus. They know that Coriolanus will remove their power if he becomes Consul, so they intend to play on his short temper to prevent him from gaining more honours, and to make him lose those he has. To become Consul, Coriolanus must follow the customary practice of standing in the marketplace wearing a simple toga, showing his wounds and begging for the citizens' votes. The tribunes know that he hates the practice, because it means he must submit to his despised enemy, the plebeians. Brutus proposes to incite the people against Coriolanus, reminding them he thinks of them merely as mules and camels, simply to be used in Rome's wars. Sicinius agrees, adding that Coriolanus' 'soaring insolence' will make it easy to provoke his anger, and his 'fire' will inflame the people to reject him (the image in lines 227–9 is of a field set alight after it has been harvested: 'kindle their dry stubble').

A Messenger brings news of Coriolanus' rapturous reception by every social class of Rome:

> The dumb men throng to see him and the blind
> To hear him speak. Matrons flung gloves,
> Ladies and maids their scarves and handkerchiefs,
> Upon him as he passed. The nobles bended
> As to Jove's statue, and the commons made
> A shower and thunder with their caps and shouts.
> I never saw the like.   *(lines 233–9)*

Brutus and Sicinius decide to go to the Capitol to watch and listen, firm in their resolve to secure Coriolanus' ruin.

Act 2 Scene 2

To create the impression that Scene 2 is set in the Capitol, Shakespeare begins with two officers laying cushions for the senators to sit on. They are Senate officials, and their conversation provides further perspectives on Coriolanus and the political climate of Rome. The First Officer succinctly describes Coriolanus' character and his hatred of the plebeians:

> That's a brave fellow, but he's vengeance proud and loves
> not the common people.   *(lines 5–6)*

The Second Officer comments on the unreliability of the plebeians' love for their leaders, and says that Coriolanus knows this well and so is indifferent to what they think of him. Such 'noble carelessness' or aristocratic aloofness was cultivated by noblemen in Shakespeare's own time (see *sprezzatura*, page 81). In reply, the First Officer says that Coriolanus actively seeks the hate of the people, and lets them know it, which is just as bad as those (the tribunes?) who flatter the people to gain their love. The Second Officer says that Coriolanus fully deserves high status, unlike those who have done little to earn it but who have used only flattery and compliments ('supple and courteous'). These people have done no deeds other than doffing their caps ('bonneted') to deserve their high esteem and fame ('estimation and report'). Shakespeare's dramatic purpose in this brief episode seems to have been to underline the tribunes' failings, setting them against Coriolanus' achievements.

A detailed stage direction at line 30 offers yet another opportunity for a stage director to show important aspects of Rome. The entry of the patricians, the tribunes and lictors (attendants on Roman magistrates), and Coriolanus and Cominius invites a display of power and social relationships in Rome. The patricians have come from a meeting of the Senate in which they have 'determined of the Volsces' (decided about their defeated enemy). Now they are about to have an 'after-meeting' to honour Coriolanus. The First Senator invites Cominius to testify to what Coriolanus has done, and hopes that the tribunes will advise the plebeians to agree to what will now be decided (that Coriolanus be made Consul).

Sicinius seems to make a courteous response, but his words have also been described as an 'oily lie'. Brutus is more direct, and criticises Coriolanus' contempt of the people. He is rebuked by Menenius, and Coriolanus, not wishing to hear praise of his feats in battle, also flings an insult at Brutus saying the plebeians are worth nothing ('I love them as they weigh') and leaves:

> I had rather have one scratch my head i'th'sun
> When the alarum were struck than idly sit
> To hear my nothings monstered.   *(lines 69–71)*

'My nothings monstered' means 'my little deeds turned into exaggerated marvels'. It seems a typical image of Coriolanus' unwillingness to hear his battle exploits praised, but some critics have questioned whether Coriolanus is speaking truthfully, and have suggested that it is the presence of the tribunes that really disquiets him. Menenius scorns the plebeians as 'Masters of the people', a 'multiplying spawn' (mere child-breeders) Coriolanus cannot flatter, and invites Cominius to proceed.

Cominius describes Coriolanus' brave deeds as a young man, his later battles, his single-handed attack on Corioles, and his death-dealing feats in the following battle. Cominius' speech in praise of Coriolanus has been described as a eulogy, an epic poem, a heroic oration and an election address. In Greek and Roman literature, and in the drama of Shakespeare's time, there are many such speeches in praise of heroes. It is an exercise in rhetoric (the art of persuasion) to persuade the hearers of Coriolanus' bravery. Cominius' theme is bravery:

> It is held
> That valour is the chiefest virtue and
> Most dignifies the haver.   *(lines 77–9)*

Cominius describes Coriolanus' feats as a sixteen-year-old in his first battle against the tyrant Tarquin who had 'made a head for Rome' (recruited an army against Rome). So young that he had not yet developed facial hair ('Amazonian chin'), Coriolanus defeated bearded soldiers ('bristled lips'). He fought seventeen later battles, and performed superhuman deeds at Corioles. The imagery is of an inexorable force, strikingly fierce and bloody:

> As weeds before
> A vessel under sail, so men obeyed
> And fell below his stem. His sword, death's stamp,
> Where it did mark, it took; from face to foot
> He was a thing of blood . . .   *(lines 99–103)*

In other memorable images, Cominius describes how Coriolanus entered the city alone and painted it 'With shunless destiny' (covered it in blood as its unavoidable fate), and later 'struck / Corioles like a planet' (thunderbolt). The result was 'perpetual spoil' (endless slaughter). It is an awesome, inhuman catalogue of Coriolanus' destructiveness, and is testament to the central values of Rome.

Cominius goes on to praise Coriolanus' contempt for material gain. For him, the spoils of war were 'The common muck of the world' (line 120). He is dedicated only to action. Coriolanus is called in and offered the consulship. Menenius adds the requirement that to gain approval as Consul, Coriolanus must speak to the people. But Coriolanus is filled with horror at the thought of having to obey the tradition of Rome and appear before the citizens in the marketplace, unarmed ('naked') and dressed only in a simple gown, show the people his wounds, and ask for their approval ('suffrage', 'voices'). He detests the thought of having to beg the approval of the people, and hates the thought of the part he must perform (there are many images of acting and role-playing throughout the play, see page 88):

> ~~It is a part~~
> That I shall blush in acting, and might well
> Be taken from the people.   *(lines 139–41)*

Brutus' immediate aside to Sicinius 'Mark you that' shows he has taken note of Coriolanus' wish that the people's right to approve the Consul might be taken away. The tribunes have registered yet another complaint they can later make against Coriolanus, who continues with his contemptuous refusal to show his wounds to the common people:

> To brag unto them 'Thus I did, and thus',
> Show them th'unaching scars, which I should hide,
> As if I had received them for the hire
> Of their breath only!   *(lines 142–5)*

Menenius urges Coriolanus not to be obstinate about the plebeians' voting rights ('Do not stand upon't'), and again recommends Coriolanus as Consul. The senators unanimously agree and wish 'all joy and honour' to Coriolanus. Once again the two tribunes remain behind at the end of a scene to plan trouble for Coriolanus. Sicinius predicts that Coriolanus, even as he canvasses the plebeians' votes, will show his contempt for their right to vote. Brutus intends to tell the plebeians what has happened and the two men leave for the marketplace.

Act 2 Scene 3

In the marketplace, the citizens discuss whether they will support Coriolanus. The First and Third Citizens appear to feel that they must follow custom and give their approval to Coriolanus. If he shows his wounds, it would be ungrateful not to support him for the consulship. They joke on their many-headedness, liable to fly off in every direction. The Third Citizen takes the opportunity to laugh at the stupidity of the Second Citizen, 'a blockhead', caught up in a fog. Shakespeare seems to be portraying the lack of unity among the plebeians, but he also shows that most seem willing to support Coriolanus if he follows the tradition of showing his wounds. They notice him entering, and resolve to speak to him individually or in twos or threes.

Coriolanus is wearing 'a gown of humility' (simple robe), the traditional garment for someone who seeks the people's voices. But it is immediately clear that he is enraged at having to speak to the common people. He parodies what he might say to the plebeians as he begs for their votes. In performance Coriolanus often uses a whining, mocking tone to express his contempt:

> What must I say?
> 'I pray, sir'? Plague upon't, I cannot bring
> My tongue to such a pace. 'Look, sir, my wounds.
> I got them in my country's service, when
> Some certain of your brethren roared and ran
> From th'noise of our own drums.'　　　　　(lines 43–8)

Menenius pleads that Coriolanus must not speak like that, but ask the plebeians 'To think upon you'. The expression provokes another outburst of rage from Coriolanus, perhaps because in Shakespeare's time beggars often used the expression 'Think upon me', meaning 'think kindly of me and give me a small coin'. Menenius again begs him to speak 'In wholesome manner' so as not to spoil his chances. But he evokes only a dismissive comment from Coriolanus:

> Bid them wash their faces
> And keep their teeth clean.　　　　　(lines 54–5)

The citizens now approach Coriolanus a few at a time, and he makes clear that he has no wish to beg for votes. But he does ask them to name the price for which they will elect him Consul. The First Citizen's reply is succinct – that Coriolanus should ask without arrogance:

> The price is to ask it kindly.　　　　　(line 67)

Coriolanus responds (with obvious contempt), 'Kindly, sir, I pray let me ha't', and promises to show his wounds in private. He quickly dismisses the first three citizens, who are puzzled by his words and behaviour. The next two citizens fare no better. The Fourth Citizen acknowledges that Coriolanus has punished the enemies of Rome, but also reminds him of his hate for the people. Coriolanus replies that the people love flattery, so he will flatter them.

Coriolanus hates the thought that he must act out a part, concealing his true nature, in order to gain the people's approval as Consul. He tells the citizens as much, saying that since the people want the appearance rather than reality ('my hat than my heart'), he will act courteously, doffing his hat ('be off to them') and so imitate the flattery of an insincere politician ('counterfeit the bewitchment of some popular man'). Sarcastically using that flattery, he concludes 'Therefore, beseech you I may be consul.' His irony and contempt are clear to a theatre audience, and he refuses to show his wounds, but the citizens seem convinced and wish him joy.

Briefly alone on stage, Coriolanus condemns the custom that requires him to beg the plebeians' approval (the 'voices' of 'Hob and Dick'). Such empty rituals obscure the truth, making him put on a hypocritical act ('fool it so'):

> Most sweet voices!
> Better it is to die, better to starve,
> Than crave the hire which first we do deserve.
> Why in this wolvish toge should I stand here
> To beg of Hob and Dick that does appear
> Their needless vouches? *(lines 98–103)*

But Coriolanus resolves to continue to beg, even though he thinks it an empty charade. Other citizens appear, and in what seems to be a sing-song mocking tone, Coriolanus begs their voices (using seven scornful repetitions of 'voices' in lines 111–17). The citizens are fooled and agree to support him as Consul:

> Amen, amen. God save thee, noble consul! *(line 122)*

The citizens leave and Coriolanus sneers 'Worthy voices.' The 'voices' episode, which began at line 1, ends with the departure of the citizens. Menenius is pleased with the outcome, and Sicinius says that Coriolanus has fulfilled the requirements to be elected Consul. He now only needs approval by the Senate. It looks as if Coriolanus will indeed become Consul. Menenius says all that is now left to do is for

Coriolanus to wear the official insignia and immediately meet the senators ('Remains / That, in th'official marks . . . senate'). Sicinius acknowledges that 'The people do admit you'. Coriolanus and Menenius leave, and Sicinius sees confidence in Coriolanus' expression: ''Tis warm at's heart'. But the entry of the plebeians, and what they say, gives the tribunes the opportunity they want to deny Coriolanus the consulship.

The plebeians report that they were mocked by Coriolanus, and that he refused to show his wounds. The Third Citizen mimics Coriolanus' scornful behaviour, recognising it as mere mockery. Brutus and Sicinius begin to lecture the citizens, chiding them for not seeing through Coriolanus' feigning. They had 'lessoned' and 'fore-advised' (taught earlier) the citizens, instructing them how to behave towards Coriolanus in the marketplace. Now the citizens have given him their votes, it seems likely he will become Consul, with 'potency and sway' (power and control). If only the Citizens could have aroused his anger ('choler'), regrets Sicinius, that would have enabled them to have 'passed him unelected'.

The tribunes now work on the citizens' emotions, choosing their words carefully to remind them that Coriolanus asked for their votes contemptuously:

BRUTUS   Did you perceive
     He did solicit you in free contempt
     When he did need your loves, and do you think
     That his contempt shall not be bruising to you
     When he hath power to crush? Why, had your bodies
     No heart among you? Or had you tongues to cry
     Against the rectorship of judgement?
SICINIUS   Have you
     Ere now denied the asker, and now again,
     Of him that did not ask but mock, bestow
     Your sued-for tongues?   *(lines 185–94)*

The tribunes are successful. Their words provoke an angry response:

     He's not confirmed. We may deny him yet.   *(line 195)*

The Third Citizen's assertion shows that Coriolanus' election has yet to be ratified by approval of the Senate. The other citizens vow to gather large numbers of their friends to reject Coriolanus at the meeting at the senate house. The tribunes plan how that rejection can be done. They take turns to plot the tactics the citizens can use:

- Tell your friends that Coriolanus will treat them like dogs.
- Gather your friends to deny your earlier vote.
- Tell of Coriolanus' pride, and hatred of you.
- Remind them of his contempt in begging for votes.
- Tell how your regard for his bravery led you to mistake his bearing ('portance').
- Blame us, the tribunes, for making you choose him.
- Say that you really wished to vote against him, but we prevented you.
- Say we told you of his service to his country, his noble ancestry, and that we recommended him to you.

It is cunning political persuasion, and Sicinius provides the clinching move for the citizens:

> but you have found,
> Scaling his present bearing with his past,
> That he's your fixèd enemy, and revoke
> Your sudden approbation.   *(lines 234–7)*

The tribunes' plan works, as the citizens agree to follow their instructions. They leave to collect more plebeians and go to the Capitol to oppose Coriolanus' election. Yet again the tribunes are together alone on stage at the end of a scene. Pleased with the success of turning the people against Coriolanus, they plan to exploit his anger to ensure his overthrow:

> If, as his nature is, he fall in rage
> With their refusal, both observe and answer
> The vantage of his anger.   *(lines 244–6)*

Act 2: Critical review

The act opens with Menenius trying to outmanoeuvre and mock the tribunes, to make them feel small. It may seem a slight, 'comic' episode (signified by the use of prose) but it has historical and dramatic significance. The tribunes are political officials whose duties included judging legal cases, so perhaps Shakespeare is making a private joke about magistrates in the City of London. Dramatically, Menenius' outburst against Brutus and Sicinius expresses a major theme of the play. He is parodying the disorder that will result if the tribunes and plebeians gain political control.

Coriolanus' triumphal entry poses a crucial performance question for every actor playing the role: how does he greet his mother and wife? This is the first time that Coriolanus is seen with his family, and the actor must decide whether Coriolanus displays any tenderness. Many productions have had him flinching from any public display of affection. Coriolanus' behaviour in this episode can give the audience a further clue to his personality. It can also throw light on how he behaves in the climactic meeting with Volumnia and Virgilia in the final act of the play.

The 'voices' episode in Scene 3 shows how Coriolanus follows the tradition in which every candidate chosen by the Senate for a consulship was required to seek the approval of the ordinary people of Rome. The procedure was not like the voting practices in modern democratic states, but rather a general show of approval when the would-be Consul appeared in a simple robe before the people to ask for their 'voices': signs of agreement. Coriolanus' contempt for the procedure and the people is all too evident throughout. He despises any thought of democracy or of using his wounds as political bribes. His disdain and anger will have disastrous results in the following act. The successful soldier is already failing as a politician.

Shakespeare's dramatic construction is again evident as he keeps the tribunes alone on stage at the end of each scene. The device underlines the dramatic importance of their role as they plot Coriolanus' downfall by manipulating the plebeians and exploiting the warrior-hero's 'nature': his explosive temper if he feels his honour or will are put into question.

Act 3 Scene 1

The simmering conflict between Coriolanus and the people will boil over in this scene. It begins with Coriolanus on his way from the Capitol to the marketplace. There the final approval of his election as Consul should take place, as the citizens confirm their earlier vote. But Coriolanus' first words are about his military rival, the Volscian leader, Aufidius. He expects another invasion by the Volsces, but Cominius says they are too battle-weary. Coriolanus is eager for news of Aufidius, and Lartius speaks of Aufidius' anger at the loss of Corioles, his past bloody encounters with Coriolanus, his hatred of him, and his hope that he might one day slay Coriolanus. Learning that Aufidius lives at Antium, Coriolanus speaks an unwittingly prophetic line:

> I wish I had a cause to seek him there   *(line 19)*

In view of what will happen in Act 3, Coriolanus' line 19 is full of dramatic irony. He is unaware that he will soon have a cause to go to Antium to find Aufidius. Coriolanus' wish will come true in a way he does not expect, but the entry of the tribunes provokes a more immediate hatred:

> Behold, these are the tribunes of the people,
> The tongues o'th'common mouth. I do despise them,
> For they do prank them in authority
> Against all noble sufferance.   *(lines 21–4)*

Whether or not the tribunes hear Coriolanus' contempt is unclear (each production makes its own decision), but Sicinius' first words are, for Coriolanus, a shocking order: 'Pass no further.' Coriolanus can scarcely believe his ears, as Brutus and Sicinius, intent on exploiting Coriolanus' fiery temper, seek to goad him into rash speech and action, and so display his unfitness to rule. They report the plebeians' anger against Coriolanus, and that they refuse to support him for the consulship. Sure enough, Coriolanus immediately explodes:

> Are these your herd?
> Must these have voices, that can yield them now
> And straight disclaim their tongues?   *(lines 34–6)*

Coriolanus claims that this is a plot against the patricians to curb their power. Brutus reminds him of how he had recently mocked the people and insulted their tribunes, calling them 'Time-pleasers, flatterers, foes to nobleness'. After an exchange of insults, in which Coriolanus mockingly declares that if he acted like Brutus he would deserve to be only a tribune, Sicinius advises Coriolanus to behave courteously. Menenius and Cominius try to calm the growing storm, but Coriolanus, enraged among other things by the mention of corn (see pages 8, 76), insists on speaking. He launches into a tirade of abuse, describing the people as a changeable, stinking mob ('mutable, rank-scented meinie'– line 67) and as a disease that produces scabs ('measles', 'tetter'). He claims that treating the plebeians kindly only produces rebellion:

> In soothing them, we nourish 'gainst our senate
> The cockle of rebellion, insolence, sedition,
> Which we ourselves have ploughed for, sowed, and scattered
> By mingling them with us   *(lines 70–3)*

Coriolanus is using corn-growing imagery, calling the plebeians 'cockle' (a weed growing among the corn: see the parable of the wheat and tares in the King James version of the Bible, Matthew 13, verses 24–30). He refuses to be silent, reminding the tribunes that just as he fearlessly shed his blood for Rome, so he will fearlessly speak his mind. The tribunes rebuke him. Brutus declares that Coriolanus speaks as if he were a stern god, not a man with weaknesses like other men. Coriolanus again indignantly asserts he will speak his mind. His assertion prompts Sicinius to use disease imagery to imply Coriolanus will be denied the consulship:

> It is a mind
> That shall remain a poison where it is,
> Not poison any further.   *(lines 87–9)*

Sicinius' word 'shall' in line 88 provokes an outraged response from Coriolanus. He is infuriated by hearing a tribune dare to give orders, and the insulting 'shall' echoes through the long condemnation that follows his initial eruption:

> 'Shall remain'?
> Hear you this Triton of the minnows? Mark you
> His absolute 'shall'? *(lines 89–91)*

In Greek mythology Triton was a minor sea god who blew a trumpet to announce Poseidon, the chief sea god. Coriolanus' insult means something like 'captain of the small fry' (minnows are tiny fish). Stung by hearing a tribune daring to issue an order ('shall'), Coriolanus first repeats and ridicules the word, then launches into three long speeches against what he sees as the dangers of democracy. The first speech is addressed to his fellow patricians, warning them that if they give any power to the people, they will lose all of their own. Divisions in the state will lead to destruction.

Coriolanus uses images he knows will have a strong effect on the patricians: the people as a many-headed monster; the people stealing the patricians' power; the thought that the people will sit beside the patricians in the Senate and their 'voice' will overwhelm the patricians. He ends with a political lesson about the need for hierarchy: that if there is not a single, supreme power, then competing factions will destroy each other:

> my soul aches
> To know, when two authorities are up,
> Neither supreme, how soon confusion
> May enter 'twixt the gap of both and take
> The one by th'other. *(lines 109–13)*

The speech is a rhetorical exercise, and each recurring 'shall' is spoken disdainfully. In the pendulum-like, swinging rhythm of the speech, Coriolanus constantly contrasts words and thoughts: 'good' / 'unwise', 'grave' / 'reckless', 'you' / 'his', 'If you are learned' / 'if you are not', 'You are plebeians / If they be senators', 'And such a one' / 'against a graver bench', 'The one by th'other'.

Cominius and Menenius again try to calm the situation, but the tribunes and Coriolanus are inflamed against each other. Coriolanus now embarks on a long diatribe (lines 120–40) against the plebeians, accusing them of cowardice and mutiny, and saying they will claim that the patricians fear them. Coriolanus gives reasons for why he detests the plebeians and why they do not deserve free corn ('corn gratis'). At times of crisis ('when the navel of the state was touched') they would not come out fighting for Rome ('thread the gates'); as soldiers, they mutinied; they complain without reason ('All cause unborn'); and they claim that the patricians fear them because they are the majority ('greater poll'). To give in to the plebeians disgraces the patricians' right to rule in the Senate ('The nature of our seats'), soon allowing inferiors to attack superiors:

> . . . which will in time
> Break ope the locks o'th'senate and bring in
> The crows to peck the eagles.   *(lines 138–40)*

Ignoring Menenius' caution ('Come, enough') and Brutus' condemnation ('Enough, with over-measure'), Coriolanus launches into his third diatribe. He implores the senators to dismiss the tribunes, and end moves towards democracy. Coriolanus returns to his condemnation of any kind of democracy or divided authority ('double worship'). He claims that such power-sharing, in which the patricians cannot rule without the approval of the mob ('general ignorance'), results in the neglect of important issues ('Real necessities') in favour of constantly changing trivialities ('unstable slightness'), with nothing worthwhile achieved.

He flatters the patricians, saying they are wise rather than cowardly ('less fearful than discreet'). They love Rome and hate to see it changed, they prefer honour before life itself, and they wish to cure Rome of its diseases even though the medicine is risky ('dangerous physic'). He begs them to rid themselves of the tribunes, 'pluck out / The multitudinous tongue' (the voice of the people), who enjoy the power ('lick / The sweet') which is poisonous to the state. Not to do so is dishonourable and unwise, because it removes the unity of Rome ('bereaves the state / Of that integrity') which dignifies it ('become't'), because the evil plebeians ('th'ill') prevent the patricians from doing good.

Coriolanus' impassioned rhetoric serves only to condemn him in the eyes of the tribunes. They have succeeded in their plan to provoke his anger, and now Sicinius, prompted by Brutus, delivers judgement, emphasising the 'shall' that so infuriates Coriolanus. He adds insult to injury by calling Coriolanus 'traitor':

| BRUTUS | He's said enough. |
| SICINIUS | He's spoken like a traitor and shall answer |

As traitors do.   *(lines 162–4)*

Sicinius' accusation provokes another outburst from Coriolanus who claims that the tribunes were appointed at a time of rebellion 'When what's not meet but what must be was law': when what was right ('meet') was overwhelmed by sheer force ('must be'). They should now be dismissed. Brutus and Sicinius feel that Coriolanus has played into their hands, and they call for his arrest. Coriolanus resists, threatens Sicinius, who has seized him, and general confusion follows as 'a rabble of plebeians' enter and cry 'Down with him! Down with him!' As the senators move to protect Coriolanus, Shakespeare provides a memorable stage direction:

> *They all bustle about Coriolanus*   (following *line 186*)

In performance the bustle is sometimes presented as a riot, with everyone on stage milling around in a furious brawl. At other times it is played as the patricians and plebeians squaring up to each other in two very distinct groups. But Shakespeare keeps Coriolanus silent as the senators and citizens squabble. In one production he sat, silent and still, contemptuously watching the commotion around him.

Menenius and the aediles try to to restore order, but Sicinius, working on the plebeians' emotions, accuses Coriolanus of wishing to remove the people's rights. Menenius describes his words as inflammatory, and the First Senator claims such language will 'unbuild the city'. Sicinius seizes upon the senator's language, and delivers one of the key lines of the play:

> What is the city but the people?   *(line 200)*

The plebeians immediately support his assertion, 'True. The people are the city.' Brutus uses their support to remind the patricians that the tribunes are the people's legal representatives, appointed with their full consent. Ignoring Cominius' objection that chaos will result, the tribunes order Coriolanus' immediate death:

> Therefore lay hold of him.
> Bear him to th'rock Tarpeian, and from thence
> Into destruction cast him.   *(lines 214–16)*

The Tarpeian rock is a high cliff on Rome's Capitoline Hill. Traitors were executed by being flung from the rock. The plebeians call on Coriolanus (who they still call Martius) to submit, but Menenius appeals for calm. Brutus is unmoved and orders Coriolanus' removal to execution. At this point Coriolanus draws his sword, taunts the plebeians and invites them to fight. Although the plebeians continue to cry for Coriolanus' downfall, he forces them away. Only Coriolanus and his fellow patricians are left on stage. His friends urge him to return to his house, but Coriolanus, still full of fury, speaks contemptuously of the plebeians as mere animals, born like pigs or cattle, 'littered' and 'calved' (lines 241 and 242).

Cominius urges caution, warning that the plebeians' rage will destroy all order. Menenius adds his own plea, using a vivid image to express that the trouble must be resolved in some way, 'This must be patched / With cloth of any colour.' Coriolanus leaves (in performance, often very reluctantly); a patrician claims he has destroyed all chance of becoming Consul, and Menenius provides a perceptively accurate description of his inflexible character:

> His nature is too noble for the world.
> He would not flatter Neptune for his trident
> Or Jove for's power to thunder. His heart's his mouth.
> What his breast forges, that his tongue must vent,
> And, being angry, does forget that ever
> He heard the name of death.   *(lines 257–62)*

The tribunes and the plebeians return, intent on Coriolanus' instant execution. The tribunes scorn the thought of Coriolanus as Consul and are determined to kill him. Menenius tries to calm them and to defend Coriolanus. But Menenius finds himself in a tight corner: he himself is under threat. Sicinius accuses him of helping Coriolanus to escape ('make this rescue' – line 280). In Shakespeare's time, 'rescue' was a legal term for assisting the escape of a prisoner, for which the penalty could be death.

Menenius, clearly aware of the danger, uses all his debating skill to try to placate the tribunes. He variously flatters the tribunes and the plebeians, and appeals to traditional authorities (gods, Rome, parents). He claims that if Coriolanus is killed, Rome would be like an 'unnatural dam' (cruel mother) who eats her own children. (His reference to 'Jove's own book' has puzzled scholars. It may be some kind of roll of honour, kept in the Temple of Jupiter (Jove) on the Capitoline Hill, recording the names of famous people in Rome's history, 'her deservèd children'.) Menenius praises Coriolanus' service to Rome at great personal cost. He implies that Rome is united, and warns of the shame ('brand') that might come on his hearers if they execute Coriolanus. But Sicinius abruptly rejects Menenius' praise of Coriolanus as nonsense:

> This is clean kam. *(line 309)*

The tribunes are determined that Coriolanus must die, and Menenius again uses all his persuasive powers to protect his friend and hero. Earlier in the scene, Menenius had said that the quarrel between Coriolanus and the plebeians 'must be patched / With cloth of any colour'. Now he tries to do that patching up, urging caution rather than speed, and that to avoid civil war with Roman fighting Roman, they should 'Proceed by process' (line 319 – by due process of law). Menenius tells that Coriolanus was raised to be a soldier, and that he cannot use refined ('bolted') language. He urges that Coriolanus should have a fair trial – that may result in death.

Menenius' pleading succeeds, and Sicinius drops his demand for Coriolanus' instant death, agreeing instead to a lawful trial. Menenius promises to bring Coriolanus to the public hearing in the marketplace.

Act 3 Scene 2

Coriolanus enters speaking to some fellow patricians. He refuses to change his attitude to the plebeians, whatever punishment they might inflict on him: total destruction, being tied to a wheel and having his bones broken, being dragged behind wild horses or flung over an infinitely high cliff. Volumnia enters, but Coriolanus does not seem at first to direct his words towards her. He wonders why she does not fully approve of his actions, particularly in view of her own contemptuous attitude to the plebeians:

To call them woollen vassals, things created
To buy and sell with groats, to show bare heads
In congregations, to yawn, be still, and wonder
When one but of my ordinance stood up
To speak of peace or war.   *(lines 10–14)*

Scene 2 is centrally concerned with whether or not Coriolanus should stay true to his nature. He asks his mother if she would 'have me / False to my nature' rather than having him 'play / The man I am'. Volumnia rebukes her son, and wishes he had disguised his true nature. She urges him to take advice in this time of crisis, and to use both honour and political trickery. In a succession of speeches she argues that it would be better if Coriolanus did conceal his true nature. Even though Volumnia has brought up her son to be the man he is, rigidly following a strict code of military honour, she now wishes him to dissemble, to combine 'policy' (political trickery, stratagems) with 'Honour' (line 43). Her arguments can be summarised:

Lines 20–4. If you had only disguised your true nature, you could have prevented the now powerful tribunes from thwarting you.

Lines 29–32. Accept advice. I'm as stubborn as you, but I use my intelligence better.

Lines 40–6. You are inflexible, a noble quality, but unhelpful when crises threaten. So combine honour with trickery in peace, just as you do in war.

Menenius supports Volumnia's pleading, and she goes on to urge Coriolanus to be deceitful, and speak insincerely to the people, just as she or any patrician would do, when necessary, to support her class. (Notice the paradox: she is urging Coriolanus to compromise, but she has spent her whole life telling him never to bend, or adjust to other people.) Volumnia's advice to Coriolanus ('seem / The same you are not' – use deceit) is followed by her using many different expressions and examples of deceit ('seem', 'policy', 'not by your own instruction', etc.) as she urges Coriolanus to be false. She makes her own position clear:

I would dissemble with my nature where
My fortunes and my friends at stake required
I should do so in honour.   *(lines 63–5)*

Volumnia instructs Coriolanus in the gestures he should make when he speaks to the people:

> Go to them, with this bonnet in thy hand,
> And thus far having stretched it – here be with them –
> Thy knee bussing the stones – for in such business
> Action is eloquence, and the eyes of th'ignorant
> More learnèd than the ears – waving thy head,
> Which often thus correcting thy stout heart,
> Now humble as the ripest mulberry
> That will not hold the handling   *(lines 74–81)*

Her mulberry image 'Now humble . . . handling' probably means 'be soft as an overripe fruit that falls off the tree when touched'. But the key phrase is 'Action is eloquence': appearances can speak louder than what is really in your heart. Volumnia goes on to urge Coriolanus to say falsely that he will act kindly towards the plebeians in future. She knows Coriolanus would rather fight than flatter ('Follow thine enemy in a fiery gulf / Than flatter him in a bower'), but nonetheless she advises deceit. Cominius reports that an angry crowd awaits Coriolanus, and Volumnia virtually orders her son to do as she advises.

Coriolanus reluctantly agrees to act out ('discharge' – line 107) a part on behalf of the patricians, even though for himself he would rather lose his life. Volumnia urges him to perform this unaccustomed part, and Coriolanus says he will put on an act. He uses exaggerated examples of putting on a false face, saying he will become a harlot, a piping voice, a smiling villain, a tearful schoolboy and a lying beggar. His parody of acting deceitfully conveys his disdain for acting a part. But that disdain immediately results in his refusing to play a part because it will compromise his integrity ('mine own truth' – line 122):

> I will not do't,
> Lest I surcease to honour mine own truth
> And by my body's action teach my mind
> A most inherent baseness.   *(lines 121–4)*

Volumnia washes her hands of him, 'At thy choice then.' She seems to lose all patience with her son, and fiercely criticises his stubborn inflexibility ('stoutness'). She accuses him of pride, and her words sting Coriolanus back into agreement: 'Pray be content.' His relationship with his mother drives his decisions, and he once again agrees to act deceitfully when he meets the people:

> Chide me no more. I'll mountebank their loves,
> Cog their hearts from them, and come home beloved
> Of all the trades in Rome.   *(lines 133–5)*

Volumnia's response is curtly dismissive, 'Do your will.' She leaves, and Cominius and Menenius plead with Coriolanus to act 'mildly' in his encounter with the tribunes and plebeians. Coriolanus sometimes gains a burst of audience laughter as he speaks his final line, but roars out the last word:

> Well, mildly be it then, 'mildly'.   *(line 146)*

Act 3 Scene 3

Scene 3 is set in the marketplace, where the trial of Coriolanus will take place. Brutus and Sicinius will act as both prosecuting counsels and judges in the trial as they plan Coriolanus' rejection by the plebeians. Brutus lists the three accusations that the tribunes will level at Coriolanus:

- He wishes to seize absolute power.
- He hates the plebeians.
- He has not distributed the booty won in the war against the Antiates (the Volsces).

The tribunes instruct the Aedile to bring the people to the marketplace, and rehearse them in how to respond at the end of the forthcoming trial. The Aedile has a list ('catalogue') showing a head count ('th'poll') of the people. It has been collected by 'tribes' (groupings somewhat like modern electoral districts), and ensures there will be a majority against Coriolanus. Sicinius and Brutus must now ensure that the Aedile understands their instructions very accurately, so that the people will behave in the way they wish:

> If I say 'Fine', cry 'Fine!', if 'Death', cry 'Death!'   *(line 17)*

Brutus adds that the plebeians must keep shouting until Coriolanus is sentenced. The Aedile leaves and the tribunes plot to enrage Coriolanus, making him use reckless language that will destroy him. Coriolanus, accompanied by his fellow patricians, enters. He makes a formal greeting which critics have interpreted very differently, seeing it variously as 'very false', 'very sincere', and 'both false and sincere'.

Coriolanus next asks twice whether every charge against him will now be decided. But he does not get his questions answered, only Sicinius' demand that he submits to the will of the people and the judgement of the tribunes. In performance there is sometimes a long pause as Coriolanus struggles with his emotions before declaring 'I am content.'

Menenius tries to support Coriolanus, drawing the plebeians' attention to his many war wounds. But Coriolanus dismisses his wounds as mere scratches. Menenius tries to excuse Coriolanus' harsh language, but, as the tribunes hoped, Coriolanus explodes with rage at the very first charge made against him. Hearing himself called 'traitor', he reacts with fury and unleashes a torrent of abuse against the plebeians and the tribunes, beginning with:

> The fires i'th'lowest hell fold in the people!   *(line 73)*

It is just the response the tribunes wanted, and the citizens roar for Coriolanus' death, 'To th'rock, to th'rock with him!' Coriolanus is incensed by Brutus' talk of 'service' to Rome, and implies that the tribune has given no service to the state. Utterly enraged, he declares he will endure any punishment rather than ask for mercy. Death, exile, flaying or starvation are all preferable to giving 'one fair word' (line 98) to the tribunes.

Sicinius now delivers judgement 'in the name o'th'people' (line 106). On pain of death Coriolanus is to be banished from Rome. Sicinius probably takes great pleasure in emphasising the word 'shall' that so angers Coriolanus, as he ends the sentence of banishment:

> I say it shall be so.   *(line 112)*

The plebeians triumphally echo the tribunes' words:

> It shall be so, it shall be so! Let him away!
> He's banished, and it shall be so! *(lines 113–14)*

Cominius tries to intervene, saying he loves Rome more than he loves his own life or his family. But the tribunes dismiss his appeal, and once more 'It shall be so' is repeated in unison as the people cry for Coriolanus' banishment. What follows is one of the climactic moments in the play as Coriolanus, cursing the people, turns the sentence of banishment on its head, and predicts that fear, defeat and enslavement lie ahead for the Roman citizens:

> You common cry of curs, whose breath I hate
> As reek o'th'rotten fens, whose loves I prize
> As the dead carcasses of unburied men
> That do corrupt my air, I banish you.
> And here remain with your uncertainty!
> . . .
>   Despising
> For you the city, thus I turn my back.
> There is a world elsewhere. *(lines 141–3)*

Coriolanus' cursing of the plebeians and his rejection of Rome makes great theatre. Every production attempts to ensure that the lines are delivered to maximise dramatic effect. Actors spend much time exploring ways of speaking, particularly such phrases as 'You common cry of curs', 'I banish you', and 'There is a world elsewhere.' For example Coriolanus' final line, 143, has been whispered, shouted, accompanied with all kinds of gestures, and, in one production, spoken off-stage after Coriolanus has left the stage. In another production he contemptuously took off his Consul's robe and flung it at the crowd on his final line.

The plebeians rejoice that their enemy has gone, and Sicinius orders them to follow Coriolanus and torment him. The scene ends with the plebeians resolved to vex Coriolanus further, and with their praise of the tribunes:

> Come, come, let's see him out at gates! Come.
> The gods preserve our noble tribunes! Come. *(lines 150–1)*

Act 3: Critical review

Once again Shakespeare structures the play so that each scene makes a dramatic contrast with its successor. At the end of Scene 1 Menenius and the senators hope that Coriolanus' appearance in the marketplace will spare him from execution. But Coriolanus' first words at the start of Scene 2 show he prefers death to changing his contemptuous attitude to the common people. At the end of Scene 2 Coriolanus' agreement to go 'mildly' to the marketplace is immediately contrasted with Brutus' words that begin Scene 3, showing the tribunes' intention to bring down their arch enemy.

Act 3 is much concerned with 'policy', the use of deceit to gain one's objectives. The tribunes' manipulative strategies are in keeping with the rest of their behaviour, but Volumnia also now uses 'policy'. She urges Coriolanus to dissemble and put on a false face when he meets the people. Her arguments echo those of Machiavelli (1469–1527) whose book, *The Prince*, was notorious in Shakespeare's time. It is a guide for rulers and politicians, and argues that any deceit is justifiable if it keeps the ruler in power.

For most of Scene 2, Coriolanus vehemently resists such duplicity. He declares he cannot cunningly play a part. For him, such dissimulation is that of the harlot, the false 'smiles of knaves', the crafty beggar's whining plea. He feels he cannot hide his true nature which he sees as noble and heroic, 'Must I / With my base tongue give to my noble heart / A lie that it must bear?' Such hypocrisy would violate his integrity and honour. But finally, to content his mother, Coriolanus agrees to follow her advice.

The result is catastrophe for Coriolanus. Unlike other characters, for him appearance is reality, and he quickly proves unable to conceal his true feelings behind a mask. The accusation of 'traitor' releases all his pent-up bile against the people and their tribunes, and his tirades against them in Scene 1 are defiantly but succinctly reprised in Scene 3. He is banished from Rome, but, fully in character, turns the sentence on its head, 'I banish you'. His final rejection of Rome will prove ironically fatal:

There is a world elsewhere.

Act 4 Scene 1

The scene is the city gates of Rome. The opening stage direction suggests that only Menenius, Cominius and the younger men of the patrician class now support the banished Coriolanus. Some productions have accompanied this scene with the sound of the plebeians jeering at Coriolanus and rejoicing at his banishment. He is about to leave for exile, and contemptuously refers to the plebeians who have banished him, 'The beast / With many heads butts me away.' He tries to cheer his mother by reminding her of the four proverbs or maxims ('precepts') she had taught him to help to endure hardships:

> You were used
> To say extremities was the trier of spirits;
> That common chances common men could bear;
> That when the sea was calm, all boats alike
> Showed mastership in floating; fortune's blows
> When most struck home, being gentle wounded craves
> A noble cunning. *(lines 3–9)*

The fourth precept (lines 7–9) probably means 'When ill fortune strikes, aristocrats should bear its blows with nobleness.' Virgilia can only appeal to the heavens, but Volumnia curses the plebeians. Coriolanus offers more comfort to his family and friends. He urges his mother to recall her former strength, and bids Cominius not to let his spirits droop. Bidding them farewell he asks Menenius to tell the two women that it is foolish to weep at what is inevitable. He continues to comfort his mother, saying that in his exile he will be like a lonely dragon in his fen, much talked about, but rarely seen. But he makes two claims that are filled with dramatic irony (contrasting strongly with what actually happens later). At lines 32–3 he claims he will not 'be caught / With cautelous baits and practice' (deceitful traps and tricks), and at lines 52–3 he says that he will never change ('aught . . . formerly'). You will find as the play unfolds that both claims are proved false.

Coriolanus refuses Cominius' offer to accompany him beyond the city gates, and bids farewell to all. This 'family and friendship' scene can be played to present a tender side of Coriolanus' character that has not hitherto been seen. But some productions play him as still unable to relax, and visibly awkward in expressing the comfort he offers. It also presents challenges to the two women: Virgilia speaks only seven words, and the actor playing Volumnia must decide just how she might display her affection for her son whom she has always treated as a soldier.

Act 4 Scene 2

Back in the marketplace Sicinius and Brutus give orders that the plebeians return home. The tribunes see Volumnia approaching together with Virgilia and Menenius. They hope to avoid her, but confrontation follows. Volumnia curses them and questions their trickery in banishing Coriolanus. Virgilia, who up to this moment has seemed modest and retiring, joins in, ordering 'You shall stay too' as she prevents the tribunes from leaving. In one production the audience laughed as the tribunes tried to sneak out, but were physically restrained by the women. In another production Volumnia aimed a blow at Sicinius at line 22, provoking him to exclaim 'O blessèd heavens!'

The two women berate the tribunes. Both wish Coriolanus could kill them: 'make an end of thy posterity' snaps Virgilia, and Volumnia insultingly adds, 'Bastards and all.' Volumnia accuses them of stirring up the plebeians ('incensed the rabble'– line 35) and says that Coriolanus is superior to them both:

> As far as doth the Capitol exceed
> The meanest house in Rome, so far my son –
> This lady's husband here, this, do you see? –
> Whom you have banished, does exceed you all.   *(lines 41–4)*

The tribunes make their escape, accusing Volumnia of madness. She calls after them, wishing she could curse them every day. Menenius' invitation to dine evokes a memorable retort from Volumnia that aptly expresses her character:

> Anger's my meat. I sup upon myself   *(line 52)*

Volumnia's imagery of cannibalism suggests that she is so full of anger that expressing it, or dwelling on it, will destroy her ('starve with feeding'). She is consumed with anger, and Virgilia is momentarily made the subject of her rage. Volumnia snaps at her for feeble whining or whimpering, and urges Virgilia to imitate her and express her grief wrathfully (Juno was chief goddess of Rome, famous for her anger which caused the destruction of Troy):

> Leave this faint puling and lament as I do,
> In anger, Juno-like. Come, come, come.   *(lines 54–5)*

Act 4 Scene 3

Nicanor, a Roman in the pay of the Volsces, meets Adrian, a Volsce. Nicanor is on his way from Rome to Antium, the capital city of the Volsces. Scene 3 is sometimes cut in performance, but that is to lose a significant aspect of Shakespeare's dramatic construction, because the scene introduces the theme of treachery that will run through the remainder of the play. Both men are spies, and Nicanor the Roman is also a traitor, a secret agent who betrays his own country by passing on information that will help the enemy.

Nicanor reports the unrest in Rome, with the plebeians set against the patricians. The news surprises Adrian, who tells that the Volsces are preparing to attack Rome again when they think the city is divided. Hearing of Coriolanus' banishment, Adrian is pleased because it increases the likelihood of a Volsce attack even more. Nicanor emphasises Rome's present weakness, and says how Aufidius will find success now that Coriolanus can no longer fight for Rome. Adrian reveals that the Volsces have an army ready to march on the city.

Who is Nicanor? In one production, he was revealed as a Roman patrician who had appeared in previous scenes. In another production both spies were plebeians, and the director declared that his intention was to show the solidarity of the working class in both countries against the patrician class. Shakespeare leaves such possibilities open. Every new production can decide how to present the character.

Act 4 Scene 4

Coriolanus, in poor and tattered clothing, his face muffled, arrives in Antium outside Aufidius' house. He knows that his life is at risk in the city where he has made so many widows, and so has adopted his disguise. In soliloquy, he reflects on the changeable nature of the world. He argues that just as firm friends become bitter foes because of a quarrel over nothing ('dissension of a doit' – line 17 – a doit is a tiny coin), so too deadly enemies, who lose sleep in their desire to kill each other, can become firm friends by chance or by a worthless action. The thought leads him to think of his own situation. He now hates Rome and loves Antium, and if Aufidius does not slay him, he will serve the Volsces. He decides to meet Aufidius:

> My birthplace hate I, and my love's upon
> This enemy town. I'll enter. If he slay me,
> He does fair justice; if he give me way,
> I'll do his country service.   *(lines 23–6)*

In Shakespeare's plays, characters, alone on stage, often reveal their innermost thoughts in soliloquy. Coriolanus is about to transfer his allegiance to his deadliest enemy, Aufidius. But interestingly his soliloquy does not reveal just why he hates Rome (his family and patrician friends are still there) and loves Antium, the capital city of the Volsces. Again Shakespeare leaves a gap for the reader or audience member to fill using their imagination. It is not clear just how Coriolanus' argument fits his own case: is it 'some chance, / Some trick not worth an egg' (lines 20–1) that has brought him to Antium, or are his lines a justification of a decision he has already taken?

Act 4 Scene 5

Inside Aufidius' house a feast is in progress offstage, and the servants bustle about. Coriolanus enters in his tattered disguise and comments that he does not appear like a guest. The servants find his appearance and behaviour strange, and order him out, but Coriolanus refuses to leave. The First Servingman decides to send for Aufidius.

Coriolanus continues to deflect questions, and rejects further attempts to make him leave. He says he lives 'Under the canopy' (sky) in the 'city of kites and crows' (birds well known as scavengers on battlefields). The Third Servingman seems baffled by Coriolanus' words and tries to make a joke of it: daws (jackdaws) were traditionally thought of as stupid birds. Coriolanus turns the joke back on the servant, then beats him (in different productions sometimes severely, sometimes playfully). The episode has sometimes been interpreted as a comic variation on the themes of warfare and deceit, but it seems inappropriate to load it with too much significance. Perhaps it suggests that the ordinary people of Antium are as fond of jokes, as unreliable (the Second Servingman boasts he would have beaten Coriolanus like a dog) and as easily puzzled as their Roman plebeian counterparts.

Aufidius appears and demands to know the name of the stranger. The word 'name' will be repeated nine times within thirteen lines (50–62), emphasising the play's preoccupation with identity. At last Coriolanus reveals his name. It is an intensely dramatic moment as Coriolanus stands, unarmed, before his deadliest enemy:

AUFIDIUS   Say, what's thy name?
        Thou hast a grim appearance, and thy face
        Bears a command in't. Though thy tackle's torn,
        Thou show'st a noble vessel. What's thy name?
CORIOLANUS Prepare thy brow to frown. Know'st thou me yet?
AUFIDIUS I know thee not. Thy name?
CORIOLANUS My name is Caius Martius   *(lines 56–62)*

The long speech Coriolanus now makes gives insight into Shakespeare's working methods as a dramatist, because it is closely based on what Shakespeare read in Plutarch. On page 76 you can compare Plutarch's original with Shakespeare's verse version of it. Here, it is helpful to set out briefly the separate elements of Coriolanus' speech:

- I am Coriolanus.
- I have done great harm to the Volsces.
- Ungrateful Rome has rewarded me only with the surname Coriolanus.
- The dastardly patricians have allowed the cruel and envious plebeians to drive me out of Rome.
- I come to Antium not to save my life, but to be revenged on Rome.
- To further your own revenge on Rome, invade now, and I'll fight for you 'Against my cankered country'.
- Otherwise, kill me.
- You will be shamed unless you either kill me or accept me as an ally.

Such a bald summary does little justice to Shakespeare's verse and the dramatic intensity of the occasion, but it does enable you to see that Aufidius' long reply is similarly constructed, as the following brief summary shows:

- Your words remove all past hatred from my heart.
- The very gods declare you speak truthfully.
- Let me lovingly embrace you, whom I fought so many times.
- You give me more joy than my own wedding day.
- I had intended to fight you again in a coming war.
- Each night I have fought you in my dreams.
- Let's destroy Rome for banishing you.
- Now meet the Volsce senators, who are preparing for war.

Again the bald summary entirely omits Aufidius' vivid imagery and passionate feeling, but it makes the structural correspondence of the two long speeches clear. In performance the speech presents all kinds of puzzles for the actors to solve, for example:

- How long does Aufidius pause before saying 'O Martius, Martius' at the beginning of his speech? The moment can be electric for an audience, waiting to see if Aufidius reacts with anger at finding his enemy facing him.
- How genuine is Aufidius' response? Is he being cunning? Or does he, like Coriolanus, 'know not policy' and speak entirely sincerely?
- How does Coriolanus respond to the homoerotic imagery, blending the sexual with the military, that is so evident in Aufidius' tale of how they fought together in Aufidius' dreams?
- How does Coriolanus respond to Aufidius' embrace?

Again, Shakespeare leaves each new production to decide these and other questions. And every actor playing Coriolanus or Aufidius will decide on his own delivery of the long speeches, which are written in a hyperbolic style quite unlike that of naturalistic modern drama.

Aufidius makes it clear that he welcomes Coriolanus as an ally to attack Rome. In response, Coriolanus speaks only a half line, 'You bless me, gods!' (line 132). Otherwise he is silent. Aufidius appoints Coriolanus to command half the Volsce army and to decide how best to attack Rome. When Aufidius offers Coriolanus his hand just before the two men leave, the handshake will seal their alliance.

The servants are left on stage to talk about what they have heard. They comment on Coriolanus' strength and discuss the merits of their masters. Their discussion of who is the greater soldier, Coriolanus or Aufidius, hints at future competition between the two leaders. At first it is not obvious which leader, Coriolanus or Aufidius, is thought by the servants to be the greater soldier. Both servants seem wary of speaking too clearly, but they finally agree that Coriolanus is the superior warrior.

The Third Servingman enters and tells how Aufidius and the Volsce nobles honour Coriolanus. They treat him as the son and heir of the war god, Mars, place him in the most honoured seat at the feast and remove their hats before they speak to him. (In Shakespeare's time, men kept their hats on indoors. It was a mark of respect to remove your hat before speaking to someone.) Aufidius treats him as a lover and as a holy relic to worship, and the nobles give him half the Volsce army. In response Coriolanus has vowed to devastate Rome:

> He'll go, he says, and sowl (drag) the porter of Rome
> gates by th'ears. He will mow all down before him
> and leave his passage polled (cleared).   *(lines 193–5)*

In lines 210–22 the servingmen criticise peace and praise war. They look forward to marching against Rome and their lines make clear how they see the oppositions between war and peace. They claim that war is a medicine that cures the corruptions of peace, and that men 'hate one another' in peace because they 'less need one another'. War puts a spring in your step ('sprightly walking'), but peace makes swords become rusty through lack of use ('rust iron'). War is noisy ('audible'), but peace can only 'increase tailors' (because men throw away armour and buy fancy clothes). It is a depressing catalogue of differences, but it gives insight into the mercenary minds of the servingmen who think they will profit from war. The Third Servingman's final comment aptly summarises the cynical dehumanisation of war:

> The wars for my money. I hope to see Romans as
> cheap as Volscians.   *(line 222)*

Act 4 Scene 6

Scene 6 returns the action to Rome where Sicinius claims that the medicine (banishment) they have given Coriolanus has brought peace ('His remedies are tame'). Even the patricians acknowledge that banishing Coriolanus has brought tranquillity to the city where the tradesmen now sing at their work and all is friendly.

The tribunes mockingly tell Menenius that only the patricians miss Coriolanus, and Rome prospers without him. Menenius reports that there has been no news of Coriolanus; not even his mother or wife have heard from him. Shakespeare is ensuring that although Coriolanus is banished, he still remains the main topic of conversation in Rome. A few citizens enter and offer their thanks and prayers for the tribunes, who take the opportunity to criticise the absent war leader:

> We wished Coriolanus had loved you as we did.   *(line 26)*

The citizens depart, the tribunes congratulate themselves on having brought peace to Rome, and again criticise Coriolanus and his desire to rule alone as king:

BRUTUS   Caius Martius was
    A worthy officer i'th'war, but insolent,
    O'ercome with pride, ambitious, past all thinking
    Self-loving.
SICINIUS   And affecting one sole throne
    Without assistance.   *(lines 31–5)*

But the tribunes' mood of contented self-congratulation is shattered as an Aedile tells them that a messenger reports the Volsces have invaded. The tribunes say it is not true, and order the messenger to be whipped. The messenger ('a slave' – line 40) has brought bad news, and he seems likely to be rewarded with a whipping. Messengers in other Shakespeare plays get beaten because of the news they bring, for example in *Antony and Cleopatra*, *Macbeth* and *Richard III*. The long tradition of punishing messengers who bring bad news goes back to Greek plays written over 2,000 years ago. The modern expression 'shooting the messenger' shows that the tradition still continues.

A messenger appears and says he has worse news. The patricians are gathering at the senate house to discuss something 'That turns their countenances' (makes them turn pale – line 62). Sicinius assumes it is the First Messenger's report, and repeats his order that the slave must be beaten in public. But the Second Messenger has more fearful news: Coriolanus has joined with Aufidius and is leading an army against Rome, vowing revenge. The tribunes think the news a trick, and Menenius cannot believe that Coriolanus has united with Aufidius, but the Second Messenger brings worse news of the developing invasion:

> A fearful army, led by Caius Martius
> Associated with Aufidius, rages
> Upon our territories and have already
> O'erborne their way, consumed with fire, and took
> What lay before them.   *(lines 78–82)*

Cominius enters to confirm the bad news that Rome is threatened with destruction. He accuses the tribunes:

> You have holp to ravish your own daughters and
> To melt the city leads upon your pates,
> To see your wives dishonoured to your noses   *(lines 85–7)*

Cominius describes Coriolanus as a pitiless destroyer:

> He is their god. He leads them like a thing
> Made by some other deity than Nature,
> That shapes man better, and they follow him
> Against us brats with no less confidence
> Than boys pursuing summer butterflies
> Or butchers killing flies.   *(lines 94–9)*

Cominius' lines 98–9 echo the description of Coriolanus' son killing a butterfly (Act 1 Scene 3, lines 54–8), and recall an image that Shakespeare had used in *King Lear* (Act 4 Scene 1, lines 36–7):

> As flies to wanton boys are we to th'gods;
> They kill us for their sport.

The two patricians heap abuse on the two tribunes, and each mention of the plebeians is probably spoken with contempt ('apron-men' – line 100, 'garlic-eaters' – line 102, 'people' – line 114, 'crafts' – line 123). Cominius declares that Coriolanus will shake Rome about the tribunes' ears, and Menenius develops the image, comparing Coriolanus to Hercules, the Greek demigod who, as one of his twelve labours, picked ripe ('mellow') golden apples from a tree in the Hesperides, the farthest limit of the world. They assert that no one can persuade Coriolanus to show mercy to Rome. There is a hint of bitter pleasure, of 'I told you so', as the two patricians tell the tribunes of the terrors that are in store for Rome. In response the tribunes speak their abject reply in unison:

> Say not we brought it. *(line 125)*

Menenius and Cominius continue their scornful abuse of the tribunes, and Menenius blames the patricians for giving in to the plebeians' demand for Coriolanus' banishment. When the citizens enter, Menenius uses the same contemptuous tone towards them as he sneers at, tries to frighten, and roundly condemns them. Cominius has commented on the changeable nature of the plebeians at line 129, 'They'll roar him in again', and his judgement seems to be confirmed as the citizens are shown as having changed from the triumphant crowds that jeered Coriolanus out of Rome. Now they appear frightened, and seek to excuse their earlier behaviour in banishing Coriolanus. In one production of the play the citizens physically assaulted the tribunes, blaming them for their plight. The two patricians leave, with parting jibes at the plebeians and tribunes:

COMINIUS You're goodly things, you voices.
MENENIUS   You have made good work,
        You and your cry.   *(lines 150–1)*

The tribunes order the citizens to return home, and to show no fear. The plebeians leave, claiming they knew at the time that it was wrong to banish Coriolanus. Left alone on stage, the tribunes hope that the news of Coriolanus is false, but their words reveal their fear.

Act 4 Scene 7

In his camp, somewhere close to Rome, Aufidius is talking with his lieutenant. As always in the play, the topic is Coriolanus, but Aufidius' attitude to his new-found ally is revealed in his first line:

> Do they still fly to th'Roman? *(line 1)*

It is obvious that Aufidius is jealous and suspicious of Coriolanus' popularity with the Volsce troops who flock to follow him. Coriolanus has become 'th'Roman', rather than a named friend. The Lieutenant confirms the high regard the Volsce soldiers have for Coriolanus and warns that Aufidius' own reputation has suffered from Coriolanus' popularity:

> And you are darkened in this action, sir,
> Even by your own. *(lines 5–6)*

Aufidius acknowledges how necessary Coriolanus is to the Volsces' campaign, but tells how proudly Coriolanus now acts towards him – as he has always done. The Lieutenant wishes that Aufidius had not shared command of the army. He seems to be criticising Aufidius' judgement, and the actor often speaks lines 12–16 with diplomatic caution, aware that he is telling his general that he thinks he's made a mistake. But Aufidius immediately understands, and hints that Coriolanus has failed in certain duties to the Volsces. Although he has fought 'dragon-like', Coriolanus has 'left undone' (line 24) things which will cause his downfall when he is later called to account. The Lieutenant's enquiry as to whether Coriolanus will capture Rome prompts from Aufidius a powerful image of how Coriolanus will seize Rome as easily and majestically as the osprey (fish hawk) catches a fish (see cover illustration to this Guide):

> I think he'll be to Rome
> As is the osprey to the fish, who takes it
> By sovereignty of nature. *(lines 33–5)*

But Aufidius goes on to claim that, although Coriolanus served Rome well, his lack of stability caused his downfall, which may have come about through:

- pride, which comes from continued success ('daily fortune') and always infects successful men;
- error of judgement, which causes political failure;
- his inflexible nature, unable to move from war ('th'casque' – helmet) to peace ('th'cushion' – the seat in the Senate), and always imposing rigid discipline ('austerity and garb').

It is taints of these faults that made Coriolanus feared, hated, then banished, says Aufidius. But his bravery ('merit') prevented talk of his faults. In a complex image Aufidius argues that thus reputation changes according to circumstances. Different people and different times change praise into condemnation, and to praise success is to bring about its failure:

> So our virtues
> Lie in th'interpretation of the time,
> And power, unto itself most commendable,
> Hath not a tomb so evident as a chair
> T'extol what it hath done.   *(lines 49–53)*

Aufidius then uses another remarkable image to tell how one successful person is driven out by a stronger person, one 'right' by another:

> One fire drives out one fire; one nail, one nail;
> Rights by rights falter, strengths by strengths do fail.
> *(lines 54–5)*

It is clear that Aufidius sees himself as that stronger fire or nail, the greater 'right' and strength which will overthrow Coriolanus. As he leaves, Aufidius makes it quite clear that when Coriolanus has defeated Rome, he will defeat Coriolanus:

> When, Caius, Rome is thine,
> Thou art poor'st of all; then shortly art thou mine.
> *(lines 56–7)*

Act 4: Critical review

In Scene 1 Coriolanus, about to go into exile, declares he will never change nor be caught by deceit. But Act 4 undermines these claims. Coriolanus switches his allegiance to the Volsces, and declares he hates Rome. In the act's final scene, Aufidius, jealous of Coriolanus' popularity with the Volsce soldiers, plans to bring him down.

Scene 2 closes the long period of political action, set in Rome, that began at Act 2 Scene 1, in which the tribunes plotted Coriolanus' ruin. Their plan has succeeded and their class enemy is banished. But in Scene 6 news of his return at the head of a Volsce army violently disrupts their complacency. That news also serves to underline the fickleness of the Roman plebeians who had earlier 'whooped' Coriolanus out of Rome. Now they protest that they had said at the time it was a pity to banish him.

This episode provides a further example of the subtlety of Shakespeare's dramatic construction. He builds up an atmosphere of crisis by using four 'messengers' (the Aedile, two Messengers and Cominius) to create a sense of urgency and growing fear as each man brings increasingly bad news, and the tribunes hear more and more reports of the impending destruction of Rome. Rather than having a single reporter, bringing all the news at once, Shakespeare heightens the drama by using four separate 'messengers'.

Act 4 further develops the theme of appearance and reality. Coriolanus, for all his integrity and inflexibility, turns traitor to Rome. Aufidius pretends friendship, biding his time until he can topple Coriolanus. In Scene 3 the Roman spy and traitor, Nicanor, provides another telling example of the theme of deceptive appearance that runs through the play.

The act also presents further evidence on the play's two major characters. Volumnia's 'Anger's my meat' (Scene 2, line 52) precisely expresses her fiery temperament, now focused on the injustice she sees done to her son. And in the final scene Aufidius offers three possible reasons for Coriolanus' failure in Rome: his pride, his lack of judgement, and his rigidity of character which prevented him from moving from victory in war to success in politics ('th'casque to th'cushion', from the helmet to a seat in the Senate).

Act 5 Scene 1

Some time has passed since the last scene in Rome (Act 4 Scene 6), and Coriolanus and his army are now besieging the city. The Romans hope to persuade Coriolanus to show mercy, but he has already rejected his old comrade-in-arms, Cominius. Now the tribunes want Menenius to plead with Coriolanus, but he refuses to go to his old friend to beg for mercy for Rome. He expresses contempt for the tribunes, telling them to crawl on their knees to Coriolanus:

> Go, you that banished him;
> A mile before his tent fall down and knee
> The way into his mercy. *(lines 4–6)*

Cominius tells how Coriolanus rejected all names, all identity, 'He was a kind of nothing, titleless', and refused any pardon for Rome. He sees war as a way of cleansing Rome, like blowing chaff out of grain. 'Chaff' is the worthless remains (husks) of corn after it has been winnowed (using blasts of air to separate grain from chaff). No one will be spared in that purge. Menenius accuses the tribunes of bringing about Rome's destruction, seeing himself and Coriolanus' mother, wife and child as the 'grain' which will perish along with the chaff, the tribunes.

The tribunes plead with Menenius to go to Coriolanus (who they flatteringly call 'our countryman') to beg mercy for Rome. Menenius refuses, but Sicinius claims that, even if he fails, Rome will honour him, appropriate to his intention to succeed ('after the measure / As you intended well' – line 48). After some reluctance, Menenius agrees, hoping that a good meal will soften Coriolanus' mood. He seems to believe that people are more likely to be pliable ('have suppler souls' – line 56) after they have eaten, but it is likely that Menenius is assuming that his own characteristic is common in others. Shakespeare may have inserted this detail to underline Menenius' pleasure-loving but unrealistic attitudes.

Menenius leaves, and Cominius expresses his certainty that Menenius' mission will fail. Cominius describes how Coriolanus sits in magnificent state, filled with implacable desire for revenge, his sense of the wrong done to him rigidly controlling any feelings of pity:

> I tell you, he does sit in gold, his eye
> Red as 'twould burn Rome, and his injury
> The gaoler to his pity. *(lines 64–6)*

Coriolanus' sense of grievance overwhelms any feeling of compassion and forgiveness. Only his mother and wife might make him show mercy, and they are already preparing to visit Coriolanus. Cominius leaves, intending to entreat them to make haste.

Act 5 Scene 2

Menenius has arrived at the camp of Coriolanus, but the Volsce sentries are unimpressed by him. They say that Coriolanus has forbidden any more embassies from Rome. Menenius attempts to put on his patrician charm and boasts of his friendship with Coriolanus:

> Good my friends,
> If you have heard your general talk of Rome
> And of his friends there, it is lots to blanks
> My name hath touched your ears. It is Menenius.
> *(lines 11–14)*

The sentries continue to refuse him entry, and Menenius claims that his reports have made Coriolanus' mighty reputation. In lines 17–25, Menenius' description of how he has been the chronicler of Coriolanus' deeds, enhancing his reputation, is rich in imagery of books, painting, bowling and coinage. Like a modern 'spin doctor' who tries to create a favourable image of a politician, Menenius claims he has painted a glowing picture of Coriolanus. Sometimes, like a bowler on a tricky bowling green ('subtle ground') he has overshot the mark ('tumbled past the throw') – that is, he has exaggerated, getting close to approving lies ('stamped the leasing').

But Menenius' claims have no effect. The guards disbelieve him and say he cannot prevent the destruction of Rome because pleas for mercy are useless. The First Watch contemptuously asserts that the banished Coriolanus will not be deflected from revenge:

> with the easy groans of old women, the virginal palms
> of your daughters, or with the palsied intercession of
> such a decayed dotant as you seem to be *(lines 43–5)*

He orders Menenius to return to Rome 'and prepare for your execution'. The guards are Volsce plebeians, and Menenius is a patrician. That social class difference can add extra dramatic edge to the episode in performance, for example in the tone in which Menenius speaks 'fellow' and the guard speaks 'sir'. The guard's repetition of 'Back' as he forces Menenius away shows that, although he is of lower social status, he is the master in this situation. But the entry of Coriolanus with Aufidius gives Menenius the opportunity he hopes for, and he claims the guard will be severely punished for keeping him from his old friend.

The first half of Menenius' speech is spoken triumphantly, even jeeringly, to the guard, whom he seems to be threatening with execution or torture. He then turns to address Coriolanus and delivers what seems to be a carefully prepared speech, learned by heart. He begins with an exaggeratedly elaborate greeting:

> The glorious gods sit in hourly synod about thy particular
> prosperity and love thee no worse than thy old father
> Menenius does! O my son, my son!   *(lines 65–7)*

Menenius weeps, hoping Coriolanus will see his tears as water which will quench his desire to burn Rome. He claims he has come because only he has the power to move Coriolanus to mercy. Menenius ends by appealing to the 'good gods' to assuage Coriolanus' wrath – and to punish the guard who has prevented his access.

But Coriolanus is unmoved by Menenius' pleading for Rome and dismisses him with a single word, 'Away!' It is like a hammer blow, and Coriolanus goes on to assert his implacable intention to destroy Rome:

> Wife, mother, child, I know not. My affairs
> Are servanted to others.   *(lines 76–7)*

He claims that, although revenge belongs to him alone ('Though I owe / My revenge properly'), only the Volsces have power to pardon ('remission'). Ungrateful forgetfulness will poison his love for Menenius, rather than pity remember how great that love was. He orders Menenius away, but gives him a letter to mark past friendship. Coriolanus ends, as he began, with an awesome certainty as he speaks to Aufidius, asking him to witness how he has treated his former friend:

> This man, Aufidius,
> Was my beloved in Rome; yet thou behold'st.   *(lines 86–7)*

Aufidius' reply is brief, 'You keep a constant temper.' But his few words are ambiguous and ironic. The Volsce warrior intends no good to Coriolanus, and what Coriolanus hears is almost certainly not the same as Aufidius intends.

Coriolanus and Aufidius leave, and the guards mock Menenius. Every production has to solve the problem of how to present the effect of Coriolanus' rejection on Menenius. Some have portrayed him in his final lines as a broken man, pathetically trying to retain some dignity. Others have shown him as defiant and proud, giving the guards as good as he gets, as he dismisses them as worthless. The Second Watch ends the scene impressed with Coriolanus' steadfastness to the Volsce cause:

> The worthy fellow is our general. He's the rock, the oak not to
> be wind-shaken.   *(lines 101–2)*

Act 5 Scene 3

At the Volsce camp, Coriolanus plans to besiege Rome. Although they are joint commanders, Coriolanus' reputation overshadows that of Aufidius. One production began the scene with Coriolanus seated in a magnificent chair of state, with Aufidius standing beside him, recalling Cominius' description:

> I tell you, he does sit in gold, his eye
> Red as 'twould burn Rome . . .   *(Act 5 Scene 1, lines 64–5)*

Coriolanus asks Aufidius to report his behaviour to the Volsce lords, and Aufidius acknowledges him as a faithful servant of the Volsces, rejecting all Roman pleas for mercy. Coriolanus still has Menenius in mind, recognising that he has sent his old friend and great admirer back broken-hearted to Rome. He now intends to hear no more pleas from Rome, whether from the state or from private friends. But even as he speaks, a shout heralds the imminent arrival of his mother, wife, child and Valeria. The prospect makes Coriolanus fear he might break his vow to hear no more Roman pleas for mercy. He declares he will be inflexible, but his self-doubt returns.

Every production tries to present the women's entry to maximise dramatic effect. Sometimes the women are veiled, and dressed in robes of mourning or tattered costumes. Coriolanus comments on their entry, but his speeches may be delivered as soliloquies or asides, not intended for the hearing of anyone on stage. However, in some productions it is clear that Aufidius and the other watching Volsces hear all, and the fact that Shakespeare provides no 'Aside' direction suggests that is what he intended in order to further heighten Coriolanus' vulnerability and his changing moods. He begins by noting that Virgilia leads, followed by Volumnia holding his son's hand. The sight clearly moves him, but he declares:

> But out, affection;
> All bond and privilege of nature, break!
> Let it be virtuous to be obstinate. *(lines 24–6)*

As his wife curtsies to him, Coriolanus' resolve weakens:

> What is that curtsy worth? Or those dove's eyes,
> Which can make gods forsworn? I melt, and am not
> Of stronger earth than others. *(lines 27–9)*

Volumnia bows to him, and Coriolanus is struck by the pleading look on his son's face. But now he rejects tender feelings and family bonds. He speaks as if the ties of blood mean nothing to him:

> Let the Volsces
> Plough Rome and harrow Italy, I'll never
> Be such a gosling to obey instinct, but stand
> As if a man were author of himself
> And knew no other kin. *(lines 33–7)*

Virgilia greets him, but Coriolanus responds that he is a different man from the one she knew in Rome ('These eyes are not the same'). Virgilia however takes him literally, and claims the women's sadly altered appearance makes him think so. Once again Coriolanus' mood changes as he acknowledges he is playing a part, and he begs her not to plead for Rome:

> Like a dull actor now
> I have forgot my part and I am out,
> Even to a full disgrace. Best of my flesh,
> Forgive my tyranny, but do not say
> For that 'Forgive our Romans.'   *(lines 40–4)*

They kiss, and Coriolanus declares his faithfulness. But his thoughts immediately turn to his mother, to whom he kneels. She rebukes him and kneels to him, an action contrary to all his beliefs. It is possible that Volumnia may be speaking ironically in lines 52–6 in saying she should kneel to Coriolanus. But he accepts the rebuke ('your corrected son'), and uses hyperbole (exaggerated language) to show he recognises that by Roman tradition a mother should never kneel to her son:

> Then let the pebbles on the hungry beach
> Fillip the stars. Then let the mutinous winds
> Strike the proud cedars 'gainst the fiery sun,
> Murdering impossibility, to make
> What cannot be, slight work.   *(lines 58–62)*

'Murdering impossibility' means 'making all things possible'. Coriolanus greets Valeria equally elaborately ('The moon of Rome, chaste as the icicle'). His greeting of his son is similarly hyperbolic, hoping Young Martius will become a supreme soldier, 'To shame unvulnerable' (impossible to dishonour – line 73), and like a huge lighthouse withstanding all the onslaughts of the icy winds ('every flaw'). Coriolanus tells his mother not to try to dissuade him from attacking Rome:

> Do not bid me
> Dismiss my soldiers or capitulate
> Again with Rome's mechanics. Tell me not
> Wherein I seem unnatural. Desire not
> T'allay my rages and revenges with
> Your colder reasons.   *(lines 81–6)*

But in spite of Coriolanus' instruction not to plead for mercy for Rome, Volumnia does precisely that, so Coriolanus asks the Volsces to listen. She uses all her powers of persuasion in an attempt to save her native city. Relying on her son's love for her and for Rome, she employs a mixture of logic and emotional blackmail to help her succeed. She explains his family's dilemma: either Rome or he must perish. Volumnia claims that if her plea fails, he will be to blame ('your hardness' – line 91). She implies that the women's appearance reveals the sorrowful state of Rome, as does their weeping and evident fear as they see

> The son, the husband, and the father tearing
> His country's bowels out.   *(lines 102–3)*

Volumnia expresses the divided loyalties the women feel: their love for Rome, and their love for Coriolanus. They are unable to pray, because praying for the one means that the other must be destroyed. The swinging rhythm of Volumnia's lines adds emphasis to her contrasts and heightens the emotional impact she knows they will have on Coriolanus. She is appealing equally to his head and to his heart as she weighs the losses:

> Alack, or we must lose
> The country, our dear nurse, or else thy person,
> Our comfort in the country.   *(lines 109–11)*

Volumnia forsees certain disaster for Coriolanus (lines 111–25): defeat and disgrace as a traitor, or victory by killing his family. She puts the oppositions starkly:

- You will either be paraded in defeat as a traitor to Rome, or victoriously ride in triumph, but having killed your family ('We must . . . blood' – lines 111–18).
- If you attack Rome, it will be over my dead body ('For myself . . . world' – lines 118–25).

Virgilia adds her own stark contribution: and I, your wife, mother of your son, will die too ('Ay . . . time' – lines 125–7). His mother's words prompt Young Martius to claim that he will survive to fight (''A shall not . . . fight' – lines 127–8). Volumnia and Virgilia have told Coriolanus that by attacking Rome he will cause their deaths. Do they mean they will commit suicide, or be killed in the Volsce onslaught? In nineteenth-century productions Volumnia sometimes produced a knife to show her intention. Modern productions rarely show that gesture.

Coriolanus, seemingly fearful that the presence of the women might evoke tenderness in him, tries to end the confrontation:

> Not of a woman's tenderness to be
> Requires nor child, nor woman's face to see.
> I have sat too long.   *(lines 129–31)*

But Volumnia has not finished. She seeks a compromise, proposing a peaceful solution (and sounding much unlike the uncompromising Volumnia of earlier in the play). She pleads for a peace treaty, but then, in her familiar style, threatens Coriolanus with how history will destroy his reputation if he conquers Rome:

> The end of war's uncertain, but this certain,
> That if thou conquer Rome, the benefit
> Which thou shalt thereby reap is such a name
> Whose repetition will be dogged with curses,
> Whose chronicle thus writ: 'The man was noble,
> But with his last attempt he wiped it out,
> Destroyed his country, and his name remains
> To th'ensuing age abhorred.'   *(lines 141–8)*

Volumnia continues to use all kinds of persuasive arguments to make Coriolanus change his mind: flattery, scorn, his wife and child, her own feelings, accusation and shame, kneeling to him, insult, resignation, prediction. She pleads that Coriolanus imitate the all-powerful gods who show mercy in using lightning, not to destroy people, but only to split a tree. She scornfully asserts that a noble man does not harbour grudges. She points to his wife's weeping, and asks his son to plead. She berates Coriolanus for letting his mother 'prate / Like one i'th'stocks' (lines 159–60), she who had always applauded his prowess in war. Furiously she accuses him of dishonesty for which 'the gods will plague thee' (line 166).

Seeing Coriolanus turn away, Volumnia urges the women and child to kneel to him. Their supplication seems to have no effect. Coriolanus does not respond. Thinking all her pleas have failed, Volumnia determines to leave, but she delivers a final insult:

> This fellow had a Volscian to his mother;
> His wife is in Corioles, and his child
> Like him by chance. – Yet give us our dispatch.
> I am hushed until our city be afire,
> And then I'll speak a little.   *(lines 178–82)*

In an astonishingly dramatic moment, Coriolanus is moved to action, and the stage direction gives the actor the clue to how much he has been moved by all his mother has said:

> [*He*] *holds her by the hand, silent*   (following *line 182*)

In the theatre there is usually a long, emotion-filled pause before Coriolanus speaks and reveals that he realises his mother has sealed his fate:

> O mother, mother!
> What have you done?   *(lines 183–4)*

It is a moment of reconciliation, surrender, emotional dependence and defeat. Coriolanus fears that in yielding to his mother's plea for mercy for Rome he has sealed his own death warrant. He appeals to the gods to look down upon 'this unnatural scene'. The phrase has a number of different possible interpretations and may mean:

- a Roman who intended to destroy Rome;
- a soldier who goes against his nature;
- a Roman who has betrayed his promise to the Volsces;
- a conquerer yielding to a woman's pleas;
- a mother whose action condemns her son to death.

But even recognising the danger he is in, Coriolanus proposes to abandon the war and 'frame convenient peace'. He appeals to Aufidius, asking whether, in the same situation, he would have done otherwise. Aufidius' reply is simultaneously laconic, ironic and charged with latent menace:

> I was moved withal. *(line 195)*

In an aside, Aufidius makes clear that he intends to regain his power by exploiting Coriolanus' change of heart. Coriolanus declares he will not go to Rome, but return to Antium with Aufidius. He sends the ladies on their way with words that acknowledge their achievement:

> Ladies, you deserve
> To have a temple built you. All the swords
> In Italy, and her confederate arms,
> Could not have made this peace. *(lines 207–10)*

The stage empties, and each production takes its own decision as to whether Volumnia shows her awareness of the fatal damage she has now inflicted on her son.

Act 5 Scene 4

In Rome, outside the Capitol, Menenius gloomily tells Sicinius that he is more likely to displace the massive keystone of the senate house than to hear that the ladies' plea to Coriolanus for mercy will succeed. He paints a vivid picture of what Coriolanus has become:

> This Martius is grown from man to dragon. He has
> wings; he's more than a creeping thing. *(lines 9–10)*

The audience has just seen Scene 3 and knows that the ladies have in fact succeeded, but Menenius and Sicinius do not. That disparity fills the opening episode with dramatic irony. Menenius manages to make a joke about what he thinks will be Volumnia's failure: Coriolanus 'no more remembers his mother now than an eight-year-old horse'. He continues his grim picture of Coriolanus' inhuman implacability:

> When he walks, he moves like an engine, and the ground
> shrinks before his treading. He is able to pierce a corslet with
> his eye, talks like a knell, and his hum is a battery. He sits in

his state as a thing made for Alexander (like a statue
of Alexander the Great).   *(lines 14–17)*

Menenius completes his picture of the revengeful Coriolanus,
'There is no more mercy in him than there is milk in a male tiger.'
Like much of what Menenius has said so far in the scene, the line
often evokes audience laughter.

A messenger arrives and warns Sicinius of danger. His fellow
tribune, Brutus, has been attacked by the plebeians. The citizens,
fearful that Coriolanus may destroy Rome, are dragging Brutus
through the streets, threatening to kill him if Volumnia's plea fails.
Neither Brutus nor Sicinius appear again. (See page 69 to read how
one production memorably staged their final appearance.)

The mood of the scene is immediately transformed as a Second
Messenger arrives with news that the ladies have succeeded in
persuading Coriolanus to show mercy to Rome. The Second
Messenger reports how the citizens, joyful at the news of peace, burst
through the gates of Rome to greet the ladies:

> Ne'er through an arch so hurried the blown tide
> As the recomforted through th'gates.   *(lines 42–3)*

Some critics have speculated that the image comes from
Shakespeare's own personal experience. Sometimes, as he walked
over Old London Bridge, a short distance from the Globe theatre, he
saw the flooded River Thames ('the blown tide') pouring through the
arches of the bridge. The sounds of celebration, music and shouting
anticipate the spectacle of the next scene in which the ladies enter the
city, joyously acclaimed. The Second Messenger's language conveys
an impression of the musical instruments and sound effects used in
productions in Shakespeare's time:

> The trumpets, sackbuts, psalteries and fifes,
> Tabors and cymbals, and the shouting Romans
> Make the sun dance.   *(lines 44–6)*

In the theatre, the characters usually do not leave the stage at the
end of Scene 4, but turn to watch and join in the triumphal entry of
the ladies in Scene 5.

Act 5 Scene 5

The ladies are welcomed as they make a triumphal entry into Rome. A Senator makes a formal speech, 'Behold our patroness, the life of Rome! . . .', and everyone on stage joins in the cry of 'Welcome, ladies, welcome!' The scene has only seven lines, but many productions stage it as a magnificent pageant, a spectacle full of action and sound. In one such production, Volumnia suddenly revealed the tiny figure of Coriolanus' son, Young Martius, dressed in a full suit of black armour, an exact copy of that his father had worn in Act 1. It was a chilling reminder that she intended to bring up her grandson to be the same fighting machine as his father.

But a few productions have staged the entry quite differently. For example, in one, the ladies entered at night, weeping, hurrying to their homes. In another production, as the triumphal procession moved off-stage, Sicinius was seen tending the battered body of Brutus who had been killed by the mob.

Act 5 Scene 6

The action shifts to the city of Corioles. There are indications that Shakespeare began by setting the scene in Antium, the Volsce capital (and provided clues at lines 49, 60, 73 and 80), but realised, as he wrote, how much more dramatically effective it would be if set in Corioles, scene of Coriolanus' great victory (see lines 52 and 92).

Aufidius tells his attendants of his intention to accuse Coriolanus in front of the Volsce lords. Several conspirators enter and greet Aufidius, who regrets the help he gave to Coriolanus, saying he feels like a man poisoned by the charitable gifts he has bestowed on others. He knows he must find a way that can be interpreted by the Volsce citizens as honourable ('admits / A good construction' – lines 19–20).

Aufidius lists his grievances: he promoted Coriolanus, vouched on his honour for Coriolanus' trustworthiness ('truth'), made him an equal partner as general ('joint-servant'), and allowed him to pick the best soldiers. But in return Coriolanus used flattery to steal Aufidius' friends, patronised him, treated him as a subordinate, and merely rewarded him with smiles ('waged me with his countenance'):

> I seemed his follower, not partner, and
> He waged me with his countenance as if
> I had been mercenary.   *(lines 38–40)*

The Second Conspirator agrees with Aufidius' view, saying the whole Volsce army had witnessed Coriolanus' behaviour and 'marvelled at it'. He adds his own complaint: Coriolanus has cheated the Volsces out of the booty they hoped to gain by conquering Rome ('we looked / For no less spoil than glory' – lines 42–3). His words sting Aufidius into bitter contempt at Coriolanus yielding to the ladies' tears, and he vows to kill him. The sounds of drums and trumpets and the shouts of the people announce the imminent arrival of Coriolanus. The conspirators remind Aufidius that he received no such triumphant welcome, and they sneer at the Volsces who greet Coriolanus as a hero even though he killed so many of their children. The Third Conspirator urges Aufidius to act quickly, and promises that all the conspirators will support his action.

The Volsce lords enter. They have read Aufidius' letter and feel that most of Coriolanus' faults might be pardoned, but agree that his failure to capture Rome is inexcusable. Their declaration virtually seals Coriolanus' death warrant, and Shakespeare's stage direction dramatically prepares for the final confrontation:

> *Enter* CORIOLANUS *marching with drums and colours,*
> *the* COMMONERS *being with him*   (following *line 70*)

'Marching with drum and colours' (flags), and accompanied by 'the COMMONERS' (the ordinary people), suggests that Coriolanus enters in full military pomp, cheered on by the Volsce plebeians. Some productions present Coriolanus in splendid armour. To emphasise his popularity with the plebeians, in one production Coriolanus ran a 'lap of honour' around the stage, being kissed and embraced by the citizens.

Coriolanus makes his report to the Volsce lords and begins by assuring them of his continued loyalty:

> Hail, lords! I am returned your soldier,
> No more infected with my country's love
> Than when I parted hence, but still subsisting
> Under your great command.   (*lines 71–4*)

In carefully chosen language, which some critics have judged to be more like a politician's than a blunt soldier's, Coriolanus presents his achievement at Rome as a success. The booty ('spoils') exceed the costs by one-third, and he has made an honourable peace treaty with Rome. The contrast with Coriolanus' earlier style is evident, and even as he attempts to hand over the signed and sealed peace treaty it is clear that he has failed to win the expected victory over Rome. Aufidius immediately seizes the opportunity:

> Read it not, noble lords,
> But tell the traitor in the highest degree
> He hath abused your powers. *(lines 84–6)*

Aufidius knows that 'traitor' will anger Coriolanus and provoke him to a rash response. As he develops his accusation of treachery to the Volsces, Aufidius uses other words and phrases that he knows will insult Coriolanus and challenge his image of himself as a man and a soldier. Aufidius calls him 'Martius' rather than 'Coriolanus', and speaks contemptuously of his unmanly behaviour in giving up Rome 'For certain drops of salt' (line 95), the tears of his mother:

> But at his nurse's tears
> He whined and roared away your victory,
> That pages blushed at him and men of heart
> Looked wondering each at others. *(lines 99–102)*

Coriolanus, infuriated by a further insult, 'thou boy of tears', threatens Aufidius, who he has so often beaten in battle. He then mocks the Volsces, exultantly inviting them to kill him and reminding them that he single-handedly defeated the Volsces at Corioles. He abandons the political language he has so recently and briefly used, and displays all his familiar bile, contempt and pride in unrestrained defiance:

> Cut me to pieces, Volsces. Men and lads,
> Stain all your edges on me. 'Boy'! False hound,
> If you have writ your annals true, 'tis there
> That, like an eagle in a dovecote, I
> Fluttered your Volscians in Corioles.
> Alone I did it. 'Boy'! *(lines 114–19)*

Shakespeare again portrays the fickleness of the plebeians as the Volsce citizens, who only minutes before had welcomed Coriolanus in triumph, now call for his death, and remember his past deeds against them:

> Tear him to pieces! Do it presently! He killed my son! My daughter! He killed my cousin Marcus! He killed my father!
>
> *(lines 123–4)*

In spite of the Second Lord's pleas, Coriolanus is killed by the conspirators, and Aufidius 'stands on him'. All productions attempt to ensure that Coriolanus' death is staged as dramatically as possible. In one famous production at Stratford-upon-Avon the actor Laurence Olivier modelled his stage death scene on the fate in 1945 of the Italian dictator Mussolini, who was shot, then hung by his heels on public display. Olivier staged a breathtaking dying fall from a high platform, then hung suspended by the heels like the dead Mussolini.

The play now moves to its end. Aufidius offers to explain to the Volsce Senate why Coriolanus was such a danger. The First Lord decrees a dignified funeral, and the Second Lord, excusing Aufidius, resignedly declares 'Let's make the best of it' (line 149). Aufidius, expressing remorse, orders the funeral march and promises Coriolanus 'shall have a noble memory' (line 156).

Many productions have enacted with great spectacle the final stage direction in which Coriolanus is borne off stage to the solemn music of a dead march. Sometimes productions have taken up clues in the script, having a column of Volsce soldiers with trailed pikes (holding the weapons, reversed, point down), and a herald (an officer who followed the coffin) speaking of the deeds of Coriolanus. In Shakespeare's time both practices were used at the funerals of noblemen. But the Royal Shakespeare Company production of 1993 staged a downbeat, anticlimactic ending in which Aufidius struggled to free himself from the weight of Coriolanus' dead body, and held out an arm imploringly, calling on other Volsces to 'Assist' (line 157).

Act 5: Critical review

Act 5 presents its own ironic reminders of major themes and actions. Scene 5, in which the ladies enter Rome in triumph, contrasts mockingly with Act 2 Scene 1, in which Coriolanus was welcomed to Rome in victory. Here, the celebration is for Coriolanus' defeat.

Similarly, just as the tribunes had earlier prepared the citizens of Rome, telling them how to bring down Coriolanus, Scene 6 shows Aufidius plotting with the Volsce conspirators to kill him. In like manner, the Volsce people are shown to be as changeable as the Roman plebeians as in the final scene they welcome Coriolanus, then call for his death.

There is ironic contrast too in Scene 3 in the way Coriolanus greets the ladies who come to plead for mercy for Rome. Each greeting expresses the theme of constancy, of remaining true and faithful. Those declarations of constancy stand in vivid opposition to Coriolanus' own behaviour. He has not remained true, and is leading an army against his own city, Rome.

The heart of Act 5 is the confrontation between Coriolanus and his mother in Scene 3. The two previous scenes present Coriolanus as implacable in his desire for revenge. In Scene 1 Cominius describes him as 'a kind of nothing, titleless' (line 13), driven only by his determination to burn Rome. Scene 2 shows his cold rejection of Menenius. But the sight of his mother, wife and son deny Coriolanus' wish to be 'author of himself' (Scene 3, line 36) and know no kin. Volumnia's emotional coercion makes him yield. In the long pause as he holds her silently by the hand, she who created him now destroys him. And he knows that all too well:

> O mother, mother!
> What have you done?   *(Scene 3, lines 183–4)*

But although Coriolanus has been fatally moved by feelings he has suppressed throughout the play, he dies displaying the same qualities so obvious in Act 1: bravery, arrogance, contempt and defiance. Comparing himself to an eagle in a dovecote, he boasts of his single-handed victory at Corioles, 'Alone I did it' (Scene 6, line 119).

Contexts

The hugely enjoyable film, *Shakespeare in Love*, portrays a popular belief about the source of Shakespeare's creativity. It shows him suffering from 'writer's block', unable to put pen to paper, with no idea of how to write his next play. But all is resolved when he meets a beautiful young girl. His love for her sparks an overwhelming flow of creative energy – and he writes *Romeo and Juliet*!

It is an attractive idea, and the film presents it delightfully, but the truth of the matter is far more complex. Like every other writer, Shakespeare was influenced by many factors other than his own personal experience. The society of his time, its practices, beliefs and language in political and economic affairs, culture and religion, were the raw materials on which his imagination worked.

This section identifies the contexts from which *Coriolanus* emerged: the wide range of different influences which fostered the creativity of Shakespeare as he wrote the play. These contexts ensured that *Coriolanus* is full of all kinds of reminders of everyday life, and the familiar knowledge, assumptions, beliefs and values of Jacobean England.

What did Shakespeare write?

Scholars generally agree that Shakespeare wrote *Coriolanus* some time around 1608. What was the play that Shakespeare wrote and his audiences heard? No one knows for certain because his original script has not survived, nor have any handwritten amendments he might subsequently have made. So what is the origin of the text of the play you are studying? *Coriolanus* was first published in 1623 (seven years after Shakespeare's death) in the volume known as the First Folio, which contains thirty-six of his plays. It is one of the longest plays in the Folio and gives unusually full stage directions. These two features have led some critics to speculate that the play was prepared for printing either from Shakespeare's own handwritten script ('foul papers') or from a theatre promptbook.

Today, all editions of *Coriolanus* are based on the First Folio version. But the edition of the play you are using will vary in many minor respects from other editions. That is because although every editor of the play uses the Folio version, each one makes a multitude of different judgements about such matters as spelling, punctuation, stage directions (entrances and exits, asides etc.), scene locations and other features.

So the text of *Coriolanus* is not as stable as you might think. This is no reason for dismay, but rather an opportunity to think about how the differences reflect what actually happens in performance. Every new production cuts, adapts and amends the text to present its own unique version of *Coriolanus*. This Guide follows the New Cambridge edition of the play (also used in Cambridge School Shakespeare).

What did Shakespeare read?

Shakespeare's genius lay in his ability to transform what he read into gripping drama. This section is therefore about the influence of genre: the literary context of *Coriolanus* (what critics today call 'intertextuality': the way texts influence each other). There is one single text that very obviously influenced Shakespeare as he wrote *Coriolanus*: Plutarch's *Life of Caius Martius Coriolanus*.

Shakespeare found the story of *Coriolanus* (and stories for his other Roman plays, *Julius Caesar* and *Antony and Cleopatra*) in *Lives of the Noble Greeks and Romans*. Written by the Greek biographer Plutarch (approximately AD 46–120), it was translated into English by Sir Thomas North, and first published in 1579. Shakespeare's dramatic imagination was fired by what he read in Plutarch's *Lives*, and he rewrote the biographical narrative to explore the forms and pressures of his own times.

Plutarch compares pairs of famous men, telling anecdotes about their lives to illustrate a moral or historical lesson. In Shakespeare's time, North's translation of Plutarch was very popular among educated people, who believed they could learn valuable lessons from studying the lives of famous men. It is easy to discover in Plutarch some of the clues to character that Shakespeare knew he could turn into thrilling drama:

> For this Martius natural wit and great heart did marvellously
> stir up his courage, to do and attempt noble acts. But on the
> other side, for lack of education, he was so choleric and
> impatient, that he would yield to no living creature, which
> made him churlish, uncivil, and altogether unfit for any man's

conversation . . . His behaviour was so unpleasant to them, by reason of a certain insolent and stern manner he had which because it was too lordly was dislike . . .

. . . the only thing that made him love honour was the joy he saw his mother did take of him. For he thought nothing made him so happy and honourable, as that his mother might hear every body praise and commend him, that she might always see him return with a crown upon his head, and that she might still embrace him with tears running down her cheeks for joy.

Although Shakespeare followed Plutarch's *Life of Caius Martius Coriolanus* closely, he made all kinds of revisions to story and character, selecting and shaping in order to increase dramatic effect. He omits some events and invents others. He compresses historical events, greatly expands the roles of Menenius, Aufidius and the tribunes, and makes the plebeians more dramatically lively, but also much more cowardly than in Plutarch, who describes their bravery in war.

Where Plutarch stresses that Coriolanus' character was affected by neglect after his father's death, Shakespeare emphasises the crucial importance of his mother, Volumnia, in shaping his personality. He makes her far more fierce than in Plutarch's portrayal. In Plutarch, Coriolanus has two children; Shakespeare gives him only one. Plutarch blames usury (moneylending at high rates of interest) as the prime cause of the plebeians' rebelliousness, but Shakespeare makes the main grievance the hoarding of corn by the patricians.

At certain points in the play, Shakespeare follows Plutarch's prose very closely indeed, for example in Volumnia's speech to her son in Act 5 as she pleads for him to spare Rome. The following extract shows Shakespeare's 'imitation' (or rather transformation into dramatic verse) of Plutarch's prose version of Coriolanus' address to his arch rival, the Volsce Aufidius. Coriolanus has been banished from Rome and has arrived in Antium where he now comes face to face with his deadliest enemy:

Plutarch

I am Caius Martius, who hath done to thy self particularly, and to all the Volsces generally, great hurt and mischief, which I cannot deny for my surname of Coriolanus that I bear. For I never had other benefit nor recompense, of all the true and painful service I have done, and the extreme dangers I have been in, but this only surname: a good memory and witness, of the malice and displeasure thou shouldst bear me. In deed the name only remaineth with me: for the rest, the envy and the cruelty of the people of Rome have taken from me, by the suffrance of the dastardly nobility and magistrates, who have forsaken me, and let me be banished by the people. . . . let my misery serve thy turn, and so use it as my service may be a benefit to the Volsces: promising thee, that I will fight with better good will for all you, than ever I did when I was against you, knowing that they fight more valiantly who know the force of their enemy, than such as have never proved it. And if it be so that thou dare not, and that thou art weary to prove fortune any more: then am I also weary to live any longer.

Shakespeare

My name is Caius Martius, who hath done
To thee particularly and to all the Volsces
Great hurt and mischief; thereto witness may
My surname, Coriolanus. The painful service,
The extreme dangers, and the drops of blood
Shed for my thankless country are requited
But with that surname – a good memory
And witness of the malice and displeasure
Which thou shouldst bear me. Only that name remains.
The cruelty and envy of the people,
Permitted by our dastard nobles, who
Have all forsook me, hath devoured the rest
And suffered me by th'voice of slaves to be
Whooped out of Rome.
. . . make my misery serve thy turn. So use it
That my revengeful services may prove
As benefits to thee, for I will fight
Against my cankered country with the spleen
Of all the under-fiends. But if so be
Thou dar'st not this, and that to prove more fortunes
Thou'rt tired, then, in a word, I also am
Longer to live most weary and present

My throat to thee and to thy ancient malice,
Which not to cut would show thee but a fool,
Since I have ever followed thee with hate,
Drawn tuns of blood out of thy country's breast,
And cannot live but to thy shame, unless
It be to do thee service.   *(Act 4 Scene 5, lines 62–98)*

Although the original text leaves many traces, there are strikingly imaginative changes, as in the final lines where Plutarch's 'I also weary to live any longer' is transformed into the vivid image and gesture 'present / My throat to thee'. It should also be remembered that in Shakespeare's time such 'imitation' was a universally acclaimed practice. All playwrights (and school pupils) were encouraged to 'imitate', and were applauded for their ability to transform someone else's language into their own version.

What was Shakespeare's England like?

Like all writers, Shakespeare reflected the world he knew in his plays. His Jacobean audiences, watching performances of *Coriolanus*, would recognise many aspects of their own time and place. This section begins with a few brief examples of particular allusions, then provides more extended discussion of features of Jacobean England that have importance for understanding the play as a whole.

Audiences would see strong resemblances between the tribunes and London's city magistrates (see page 19). The insults that Coriolanus and the tribunes exchange echo the political language of the time.

There are mentions of contemporary events. For example Coriolanus abusively compares the reliability of the plebeians to 'the coal of fire upon the ice' (Act 1 Scene 1, line 156). The image conjures up the great frost of December to January 1607–8 when the Thames froze over. Londoners disported themselves on the ice, and one feature was bowls of burning coals, used to heat water with which barber-surgeons plied their trade. In another of Coriolanus' rants ('he'll turn your current in a ditch / And make your channel his' – Act 3 Scene 1, lines 97–8) there may be a reference to Hugh Middleton's much discussed plan to bring water to London using a new channel.

Brutus, describing how Coriolanus was welcomed back to Rome

after his victory at Corioles, relates that high-born ladies threw off their veils, risking suntans ('Our veiled dames / Commit the war of white and damask in / Their nicely guarded cheeks to th'wanton spoil / Of Phoebus' burning kisses' Act 2 Scene 1, lines 186–9). His words reflect the prejudice against tanned skins in Shakespeare's time, which were thought to be a sign of low status.

Similarly, Jacobeans would recognise everyday proverbs and fables and biblical quotations. Menenius' tale of the belly was widely known in various different versions. Elsewhere Coriolanus uses corn-growing imagery, as he rages against the plebeians as 'the cockle of rebellion' ('cockle' was a weed which grew among the corn: see the parable of the wheat and tares in the King James version of the Bible, Matthew 13, verses 24–30).

In addition to such topical reminders, there are other ways in which *Coriolanus* reveals what Jacobean England was like. Important social and cultural contexts that influenced the creation of *Coriolanus* include enclosures and corn riots, the warrior-heroes of the time, Crown versus Parliament, and the influence of Machiavelli.

Enclosures and corn riots

Like Coriolanus' Rome, Shakespeare's England was a land of 'haves' and 'have-nots', the counterparts of Rome's patricians and plebeians: the powerful and the powerless. The great majority of the people were very poor. In England's acutely hierarchical society, King James and the aristocracy clung to their privileges. Like Rome's patricians, they were obsessed with notions of honour and esteem, measured by rank, breeding and wealth.

But the power of this small elite was increasingly being challenged. A growing merchant class was becoming prosperous, and wanted to gain a share in government. Even though Shakespeare lived through a time of great social change in which England's wealth grew rapidly, one aspect of that change caused great suffering and discontent, and is reflected in *Coriolanus*: enclosures.

Throughout Shakespeare's lifetime, land which had once been common was 'enclosed': claimed as the sole property of rich landlords. The enclosures resulted in a huge underclass of landless labourers whose misery was made worse by falling wages and rising prices. Facing a lifetime of ceaseless toil and grinding poverty, the landless labourers became increasingly disaffected. They had virtually no control over their lives. In times of war they could be recruited into the army. In peace, famine was an ever-present threat.

The exploitation of the landless labourers cruelly contrasted with the prosperity of those who had enclosed what had once been common land. The conspicuous consumption and greed of the rich stood in stark opposition to the poverty and harsh conditions of life for the majority. The rich felt threatened by the poor, and used every method to control them. Evidence of the authorities' fear of such dangerous protest can be seen in a Royal Proclamation of 1607:

> Many of the meanest sort of our people . . . have presumed
> lately to assemble themselves riotously in multitudes . . . Of all
> other seditions none doth bring such infinite waste and
> desolation upon a kingdom or state than these popular
> insurrections which though they do seldom shake or endanger
> a crown, yet they do bring a heap of calamities upon
> multitudes of innocent subjects.

But resentment and protests against enclosures grew, and following a series of bad harvests, riots broke out in 1607–8 in the English Midlands. Known as the 'Midlands insurrection', the protests were directed against enclosures and the hoarding of corn by 'gentlemen'. In one riot in Northamptonshire, between forty and fifty of the protesters were killed. Shakespeare must have had first-hand knowledge of the uprisings, because at this time he was a landowner in and around Stratford-upon-Avon, and so was seen locally as a 'gentleman'. In his home county of Warwickshire the protesting labourers issued a manifesto:

> If it should please God to withdraw his blessing in not
> prospering the fruits of the Earth but one year (which God
> forbid) there would be a worse and more fearful dearth
> happen than did in King Edward II's time, when people were
> forced to eat cats' and dogs' flesh, and women to eat their own
> children . . . We, as members of the whole, do feel the smart of
> these encroaching Tyrants, who would grind our flesh upon
> the whetstone of poverty, and make our loyal hearts to faint
> with breathing, so that they may dwell by themselves in the
> midst of their herds of fat wethers.

Shakespeare would have known of 'the cockle of rebellion', and may have seen it with his own eyes: the riots find their echo in Act 1 of *Coriolanus* as the 'mutinous citizens' protest against the hoarding of corn by the patricians.

The warrior-heroes of the time

Some critics argue that Coriolanus is a portrait of Robert Devereux, Earl of Essex, a favourite of Queen Elizabeth. He was executed in 1601 for rebellion against the queen. A sermon preached in that year by William Barlow directly compared Essex with Plutarch's Coriolanus, 'a gallant young, but discontented Roman, who might make a fit parallel for the late earl'. Others claim that Shakespeare had in mind Sir Walter Raleigh (1554–1618), another favourite of the queen, and a rival of Essex. Raleigh held a monopoly of the tin mines in Cornwall, and there is much evidence that his mercenary exploitation made him hated by the miners and other ordinary citizens. He was famous for his pride and his delight in war. A contemporary writing of Raleigh in 1586 declared:

> No man is more hated than him; none cursed more daily by
> the poor, of whom infinite numbers are brought to extreme
> poverty through the gift of cloth to him. His pride is
> intolerable, without regard to any, as the world knows.

Both noblemen, Essex and Raleigh, like many of their aristocratic contemporaries, embodied the fashionable ideal for high-born males which had originated in Italy: *sprezzatura*. The term's meaning includes a nonchalant ease of manner, a studied contempt of popular opinion, and a contemptuous disdain for the poor. Shakespeare embodies that ideal in Coriolanus and the patricians. It is one in which 'nobleness' is understood as military potency, with the prime virtue of the nobleman lying in valiant bravery, his military ability and success in war.

However, in Shakespeare's England, although *sprezzatura* and the pursuit of glory through war was practised and acclaimed, it was increasingly challenged and undermined by those aristocrats who became bureaucrats and policy makers. Men like William Cecil and Robert Cecil became much more powerful than the militarists, through successful diplomacy and in seemingly mundane tasks like organising and managing taxation of the nation-state. They outmanoeuvred the less politically skilled aristocrats who clung to the older ideal that a nobleman's most important service to a sovereign or a state lay on the battlefield. Coriolanus (like the chivalry-loving Hotspur of *King Henry IV Part 1*) can be seen as Shakespeare's portrayal of an aristocrat whose ideals belonged to an earlier age and were out of place both in republican Rome and in Jacobean England.

Crown versus Parliament

Some critics argue that the conflict between the patricians and the tribunes reflects the often bitter struggles for political power between King James and the House of Commons. The Commons appealed to their right as the popular voice of the people, but the king asserted that by divine right (the will of God) he held supreme power to approve or reject laws. King James was deeply angered by the challenge to his authority, and in 1605 contemptuously spoke of Members of Parliament as 'the Tribunes of the people, whose mouths cannot be stopped'. In another echo of the play, one faction of the Commons wanted the argument with the king to be conducted 'mildly', the word which so irritates Coriolanus at the end of Act 3 Scene 2.

Shakespeare's England resembled Rome in that each comprised a small property-owning class with political power, a huge underprivileged underclass with no voting rights, and a growing 'middle class' concerned to acquire more political power. Criticism of the corruption of the Court was frequently expressed, and as in the play, the hotly debated question in Jacobean England was who should have power. In that debate (which would ignite into armed combat in the Civil War from 1642 in which James' son, King Charles I, would be executed), the example of Rome was frequently appealed to. But different factions appealed to different periods of Rome's history and constitution. King James favoured the time of imperial Rome, where one man, the emperor, held absolute power. In contrast, Parliament invoked republican Rome, in which power was dispersed. Here the divided powers of the Consul, the Senate and the tribunes provided a model for similarly divided authority between the king, the House of Lords and the House of Commons.

But in neither model were the common people, the plebeians, regarded as having a significant part to play. The modern conception of democracy still lay far in the future. However, the part that the ordinary people of Rome play in the election of Coriolanus as Consul may reflect quarrels about political elections that raged in Shakespeare's time. Election to the English Parliament was not by secret ballot, but by acclamation, a shout of assent to confirm a candidate already chosen by a tiny minority of the elite ruling group. That system was increasingly challenged around the time that Shakespeare wrote the play. In his own county of Warwickshire there was a case of the electors revoking their original approval, just as, in Act 2 Scene 3, the tribunes urge the plebeians to do.

It is also valuable to note here that the play has occasionally been seen as reflecting a different, more local, aspect of antagonism to the Crown. *Coriolanus* has been interpreted as mirroring the long-festering dispute between King James and the City of London over the right to levy taxation in the city.

The influence of Machiavelli

A few critics have read the play as strongly influenced by Shakespeare's knowledge of Italian politics, and the writings of Niccolò Machiavelli (1469–1527) whose book, *The Prince* (1532), was a handbook for rulers about the use of deceit in statecraft. Machiavelli urged rulers to use any means, however unethical or immoral, to stay in power. This opportunistic, 'Italian politics' approach can be seen in the play in Coriolanus' steadfast refusal to dissemble (a rejection of machiavellianism) and in his mother's advocacy of deceit or 'policy' to win the plebeians' voices (Act 3 Scene 2, lines 40–93). She claims there is no dishonour in Coriolanus using 'words that are but roted in / Your tongue' (i.e. spoken insincerely) and claims:

> I would dissemble with my nature where
> My fortunes and my friends at stake required
> I should do so in honour.   *(lines 63–5)*

She goes on to give her son precise instructions as to how he should behave and speak to the plebeians, and urges him to:

> be ruled, although I know thou hadst rather
> Follow thine enemy in a fiery gulf
> Than flatter him in a bower.   *(lines 91–3)*

The educated members of Shakespeare's audience would have no problems in recognising Volumnia's advice as machiavellianism in action.

Shakespeare's own life

This section began with the film *Shakespeare in Love*. It is a delightful fantasy which gives the impression that the inspiration for *Romeo and Juliet* was Shakespeare's own personal experience of falling in love. Today, critics and examiners give little or no credit to approaches which interpret *Coriolanus* in the context of Shakespeare's emotional life, because nothing is really known of his intimate thoughts, feelings or activities. The focus of critical attention is on social and cultural contexts such as those identified in this section.

But many critics have claimed that in *Coriolanus* they can detect Shakespeare's attitude to the practices, conventions and values of the time like those discussed above. They assert they can provide truthful answers to such questions as: What was Shakespeare's attitude to the common people of Rome and England? What were his views on sharing political power? And is the play a subtle critique of the aristocratic pride of some of his famous contemporaries? But being realistic, no one really knows for certain Shakespeare's own beliefs on such matters.

Nonetheless it is worth mentioning three 'personal' matters which may well have influenced Shakespeare as he wrote *Coriolanus*. The first is the death of his mother in 1608. Her death may have prompted Shakespeare to write a play that explores the relationship of mother and son. Second is Shakespeare's personal status as a 'gentleman' in Warwickshire: the class against which the riots of 1607–8 were directed (see page 80). Third is his experience as a playwright and major shareholder in the acting company, The King's Men. In 1608 the company began playing in the indoor theatre at Blackfriars, playing before an elite audience, much different from that of the populist outdoor Globe (where The King's Men continued to perform). Some critics have speculated that the opening of the Blackfriars theatre prompted Shakespeare to reflect on the theatrical implications of the troubled relations between social groups in the England of his time.

Language

Ben Jonson famously remarked that Shakespeare 'wanted art' (lacked technical skill). But Jonson's comment is mistaken, as is the popular image of Shakespeare as a 'natural' writer, utterly spontaneous, inspired only by his imagination. Shakespeare possessed a profound knowledge of the language techniques of his own and previous times. In each play he uses a range of language styles appropriate to the characters, themes and atmosphere of the play, indeed to create those characters, themes and moods. Nowhere is that more evident than in *Coriolanus*, where the harsh, gritty vocabulary, the rugged tone and the martial language ('His sword, death's stamp') create Coriolanus and the military–political world in which he lives and dies.

The language of *Coriolanus* has been described as austere, hyperbolic, devoid of lyricism, and 'language looking for a quarrel'. T S Eliot's poem, 'Coriolan', expresses its hard, uncompromising nature:

> Stone, bronze, stone, steel, stone, oakleaves,
> Horses' heels over the paving . . .

But for all its tense and metallic, violent and disruptive quality, the language is successfully put to a wide variety of dramatic usages. There is persuasion and invective, eulogy (praise) and harangue, accusation and argument, manipulation and exhortation (urging). In addition, the language of the play creates a strong physical sense of the city of Rome: halls, gates, ports, streets, conduits, temples, windows, roofs, storehouses, mills, shops and stalls. In similar fashion it conveys an impression of the bustling life of Rome's people: mechanics, cobblers, tailors, apron-men, actors, orangewives, faucet (wine-tap) sellers, ballad makers, mountebanks.

The play contains words which have now dropped out of use ('mammocked', 'empericutic', 'coyed', 'bale' etc.), and many others which Shakespeare invents to suit his dramatic purposes. For example he uses prefixes (e.g. un-) as in 'unchilded', 'unactive', 'unclog', 'unshout', 'unsaluted', 'disbenched', 'bemock', 'demerits', 'undercrest'. He turns nouns into verbs, adding to the concrete nature of the play's language: 'godded', 'virgined', 'coffined', 'agued', 'horsed', 'servanted', 'monstered'. And towards the end of the play, silence possesses its own eloquence in the remarkable stage direction which conveys how his mother's pleading for Rome has worked its fatal effect upon her son:

> [*He*] *holds her by the hand, silent*
>
> *(Act 5 Scene 3, following line 182)*

What follows are some of the language techniques Shakespeare uses in *Coriolanus* to intensify dramatic effect, create mood and character, explore political forms and pressures, and so produce memorable theatre. As you read them, always keep in mind that Shakespeare wrote for the stage, and that actors will therefore employ a wide variety of both verbal and non-verbal methods to exploit the dramatic possibilities of the language. They will use the full range of their voices and accompany the words with appropriate expressions, gestures and actions.

Imagery

In spite of its frequent harshness and lack of lyricism, the language of *Coriolanus* abounds in imagery (sometimes called 'figures' or 'figurative language'): vivid words and phrases that help create the atmosphere of the play as they conjure up emotionally charged pictures or associations in the imagination. Imagery enhances and deepens imaginative effect, creating mood and giving insight into characters' feelings and thoughts. For example Cominius' description of the plebeians 'whose rage doth rend / Like interrupted waters, and o'erbear / What they are used to bear' (Act 3 Scene 1, lines 250–2) is an image of a dammed-up river bursting its banks (and incidentally one of Shakespeare's favourite images). Only two lines later Menenius declares that the disruption that Coriolanus' anger has caused 'must be patched / With cloth of any colour' (lines 254–5). Here Rome is pictured as a torn garment to be repaired in any way possible.

Shakespeare's imagery uses metaphor, simile or personification. All are comparisons which in effect substitute one thing (the image) for another (the thing described):

- A *simile* compares one thing to another using 'like' or 'as'. Coriolanus speaks of his exile, 'I go alone, / Like to a lonely dragon', and Cominius tells how Coriolanus 'struck / Corioles like a planet', and describes his inexorable progress in battle with men falling before him 'As weeds before / A vessel under sail'.

- A *metaphor* is also a comparison, suggesting that two dissimilar things actually resemble one another. For Coriolanus, Aufidius 'is a lion / That I am proud to hunt', and Menenius vividly describes Coriolanus' expression as he refuses to hear any pleas of mercy for Rome, 'The tartness of his face sours ripe grapes.' To put it another way, a metaphor borrows one word or phrase to express another, as when Coriolanus contemptuously mocks Sicinius as 'this Triton of the minnows' (captain of tiny fish, see page 34). Similarly Volumnia describes Coriolanus in battle as a harvestman relentlessly reaping his enemies' lives.

- *Personification* turns all kinds of things into persons, giving them human feelings or attributes. Rome itself is sometimes personified (e.g. in 'whose gratitude / Towards her deservèd children' (Act 3 Scene 1, lines 296–7), as are Death ('that dark spirit'), Fortune, Custom, war ('sprightly walking, audible and full of vent') and peace ('deaf, sleepy, insensible').

Early critics such as John Dryden and Doctor Johnson were critical of Shakespeare's fondness for imagery. They felt that many images obscured meaning and detracted attention from the subjects they represented. Over the past two hundred years, however, critics, poets and audiences have increasingly valued Shakespeare's imagery. They recognise how he uses it to give pleasure as it stirs the audience's imagination, deepens the dramatic impact of particular moments or moods, creates character, and intensifies meaning and emotional force. Images carry powerful significance far deeper than their surface meanings. The following are some of the clusters of repeated images which help build up a sense of the themes of the play.

Animal imagery: 'You common cry of curs'

There are striking contrasts in the animal imagery used to describe patricians or plebeians. Coriolanus and his patrician class, the nobility of Rome, are the predators: lions, eagles, the osprey, dragon. The plebeians are the prey or vermin: hares, deer, geese, fish, mice, rascals (young deer), rats, curs. Coriolanus pictures the citizens of Rome as a hydra, a many-headed monster ('the beast with many heads'). He uses a similar unnatural image as he refuses to hear his deeds praised: 'my nothings monstered'.

Eating and food: 'Rome . . . like an unnatural dam / Should now eat up her own!'

Together with the animal imagery of predators and prey go a host of images of food and eating. The corn riot of the opening scene of the play evokes imagery of eating, and Menenius tells his fable of the belly. Volumnia rejects Menenius' invitation to dinner with the memorable 'Anger's my meat. I sup upon myself, / And so shall starve with feeding' (Act 4 Scene 2, lines 52–3). Aufidius' servant uses a fantastic image of eating to describe how Coriolanus might have treated Aufidius in Antium, 'And he had been cannibally given, he might have broiled and eaten him too' (Act 4 Scene 5, lines 183–4). Coriolanus claims that without the patricians the plebeians 'Would feed on one another', and the Second Citizen claims that war may eat up the plebeians (Act 1 Scene 1, lines 69–70), but it is war that finally devours Coriolanus. (See pages 108, 126 for how the imagery of eating underpins a psychoanalytic interpretation of the play.)

Acting: 'Like a dull actor, now / I have forgot my part'

The theme of false appearance is often expressed in images of acting and theatre. Coriolanus is unwilling to entreat the citizens for their votes, 'It is a part / That I shall blush in acting' (Act 2 Scene 2, lines 139–40). Volumnia tries to persuade him to conceal his real character and attitudes behind a friendly mask. She gives him a lesson in how to behave, urging him to 'perform a part / Thou hast not done before'. Although Coriolanus wishes to 'play / The man I am' (Act 3 Scene 2, lines 16–17), he finally agrees to go to the plebeians and 'mountebank their loves' (line 133). Later he will play the part of traitor to Rome in Antium.

Disease and surgery: 'infected with my country's love'

Images of sickness and medicine abound. Coriolanus' first words in the play express his contempt for the plebeians, who 'rubbing the poor itch of your opinion, / Make yourself scabs' (Act 1 Scene 1, lines 148–9). He heaps images of disease on his soldiers as they retreat at Corioles: 'All the contagion of the south light on you . . . boils and plagues / Plaster you o'er . . . and one infect another / Against the wind a mile!' (Act 1 Scene 4, lines 31–5). Coriolanus is himself seen by Sicinius as a 'disease that must be cut away'.

The body and fragmentation: 'tearing his country's bowels out'
Images of the body recur frequently throughout the play. They symbolise the state as the body politic, but a body fatally divided against itself. The imagery in Menenius' fable of the belly in Act 1 Scene 1 is intended to reinforce the patrician ideology of Rome as a united body, with all its parts functioning harmoniously. But the body imagery that follows exposes that unity to be a fiction, showing the body parts to be at war with each other.

Coriolanus dismisses the plebeians as 'fragments', and calls the tribunes 'tongues o'th'common mouth'. Menenius' own imagery dismembers or fragments the united body, making the plebeians merely 'voices', 'tongues', 'mouths', 'breath', 'heart', 'hands'. He calls them 'the mutinous members', and their leader 'the great toe'. Such imagery of dismemberment, like the picture of Coriolanus' young son 'mammocking' (tearing apart) a butterfly, emphasises the disunity of Rome.

Antithesis

Antithesis is the opposition of words or phrases against each other, as when Coriolanus declares 'brave death outweighs bad life' (Act 1 Scene 6, line 71), or claims 'My birthplace hate I, and my love's upon / This enemy town' (Act 4 Scene 4, lines 23–4). This setting of word against word ('brave death' opposes 'bad life', 'birthplace' is set against 'enemy town', and 'hate' against 'love') is one of Shakespeare's favourite language devices. He uses it extensively in all his plays. Why? Because antithesis powerfully expresses conflict through its use of opposites, and conflict is the essence of all drama.

In *Coriolanus*, conflict occurs in many forms: patricians versus plebeians, Romans versus Volsces, Coriolanus versus Aufidius (and almost everybody else). At the end of the play, Coriolanus struggles with himself as his commitment to his mother overcomes his desire for revenge against Rome. The antitheses that recur inexorably throughout the play are Shakespeare's linguistic embodiment of those conflicts. As the play opens, the First Citizen's lines 12–19 are full of antitheses which give a swinging, pendulum-like rhythm to his prose:

We are accounted poor citizens, the patricians good. What
authority surfeits on would relieve us. If they would yield us
but the superfluity while it were wholesome, we might guess
they relieved us humanely . . . our sufferance is a gain to them.
Let us revenge this with our pikes, ere we become rakes; for
the gods know, I speak this in hunger for bread, not in thirst
for revenge.   *(Act 1 Scene 1, lines 12–19)*

In the same scene, Coriolanus' contemptuous diatribe against the
Roman citizens demonstrates starkly how antithesis intensifies the
sense of dramatic conflict, as word is implacably opposed to word:

> What would you have, you curs,
> That like nor peace nor war? The one affrights you,
> The other makes you proud. He that trusts to you,
> Where he should find you lions finds you hares,
> Where foxes, geese you are – no surer, no,
> Than is the coal of fire upon the ice,
> Or hailstone in the sun.   *(Act 1 Scene 1, lines 151–7)*

Repetition

Different forms of language repetition run through the play,
contributing to its atmosphere, creation of character and dramatic
impact. Sometimes words or phrases are repeated for particular effect.
The repeated use of 'traitor' by the tribunes and Aufidius provokes
Coriolanus to fury. So too does Aufidius' use of 'Boy' in the play's final
scene. 'Boy' angrily evokes, with increasing intensity, Coriolanus'
three repetitions of the word in his speech of defiance of the Volsces.
More subtle, but just as dramatically effective, is the use of the simple
word 'shall' by the tribunes in Act 3 Scene 1. It tips Coriolanus over
into frenzied repetition of the word as he feels himself, a patrician,
mortally insulted at being commanded by a mere representative of the
plebeians. But the tribunes continue to goad him with their repetition
of 'shall'.

However, to Coriolanus' ears the offensive word that is most often
repeated is 'voice' or 'voices'. Used almost fifty times in the play, it
always serves to ignite Coriolanus' contempt, because it represents
what he abhors: the common people of Rome having some

democratic control over the election of their leaders. In the repetition of such apparently simple words as 'voice', 'shall', 'traitor' and 'boy', Shakespeare finds a way of further deepening crucial themes of the play: questions of power, of loyalty and of manhood.

Another form of language repetition that embodies and expresses the themes of the play are the recurring images that have been discussed above (pages 87–9), expressing the fragmentation of the human and political body, the devouring effects of war and mother love, and the disease and corruption that characterises a military state. The verse of *Coriolanus* too, with its frequent use of antithesis, also heightens theatrical effect and deepens emotional and imaginative significance through repetitive rhythms and contrasts; the same effect is also frequently evident in prose passages.

Such linguistic repetitions mirror Shakespeare's dramatic construction. That construction is not achieved simply through setting character against character or faction against faction but by setting scene against scene as they reflect each other. The tribunes are frequently left, at the end of scenes, alone on stage to discuss what they have seen and to plan their developing strategy against Coriolanus. Coriolanus' triumphal entry in Act 2 Scene 1 is mirrored ironically in the entry of Volumnia and the women in Act 5 Scene 5 in which their triumph is, in effect, defeat for Coriolanus.

Lists

One of Shakespeare's favourite language methods is to accumulate words or phrases rather like a list. He had learned the technique as a schoolboy in Stratford-upon-Avon (where different forms of the technique were given Latin names), and his skill in using lists dramatically is evident in the many examples in *Coriolanus*. He expands and varies description, feeling and argument as he 'piles up' item on item, incident on incident. For example, Menenius insults the tribunes as 'a brace of unmeriting, proud, violent, testy magistrates, alias fools', and Aufidius lists eight examples of 'privilege and custom' that he vows will not protect Coriolanus from his hate:

> Nor sleep nor sanctuary,
> Being naked, sick, nor fane nor Capitol,
> The prayers of priests, nor times of sacrifice
>
> *(Act 1 Scene 10, lines 19–21)*

The many insults and threats throughout the play can often be seen as accumulative lists, as can particular speeches, for example when Coriolanus agrees in Act 3 Scene 2 to put on an act. He uses exaggerated examples of putting on a false face, saying he will become a harlot, a piping voice, a smiling villain, a tearful schoolboy, and a lying beggar. Each 'item' is a parody of acting deceitfully, and increasingly conveys Coriolanus' disdain for acting a part.

The many lists in the play provide valuable opportunities for actors to vary their delivery. In speaking, a character usually seeks to give each 'item' a distinctiveness in emphasis and emotional tone, and sometimes an accompanying action and expression. In addition, the accumulative effect of lists can add to the force of argument, enrich atmosphere, amplify meaning and provide extra dimensions of character.

Verse and prose

How did Shakespeare decide whether to write in verse or prose? One answer is that he followed theatrical convention. Prose was traditionally used by comic and low-status characters. High-status characters spoke verse. 'Comic' scenes were written in prose, but audiences expected verse in 'serious' scenes: the poetic style was thought to be particularly suitable for moments of high dramatic or emotional intensity. So the plebeians' speeches are usually in prose, and Coriolanus' in verse.

But Shakespeare never followed any convention slavishly, and his characters switch from prose to verse, possibly depending on whether Shakespeare judged the situation to be 'comic' or 'serious'. For example, in the opening scene the citizens (low status) speak prose, but the Second Citizen switches to very formal verse to question Menenius on the meaning of the fable of the belly. In the same scene Menenius (high status) uses prose in his conversation with the tribunes. The high-status Roman ladies use much prose in their first scene at home, as does Coriolanus in the 'voices' episode in the marketplace with the plebeians. The three ladies also speak prose, as they talk with Menenius, awaiting Coriolanus' triumphal entry to Rome (Act 2 Scene 1).

Menenius also speaks prose in his conversation with the Volsce guards in Act 5 Scene 2 and with the tribunes in Act 5 Scene 4 as they anticipate Coriolanus will show no mercy to Rome. Even Coriolanus uses prose as he stands in the marketplace to appeal for the plebeians' voices. Interestingly, the tribunes (judged low status by the patricians) most frequently use verse, perhaps because Shakespeare judges most of their appearances 'serious'.

The verse of Coriolanus is mainly blank verse: unrhymed verse written in iambic pentameter. It is conventional to define iambic pentameter as a rhythm or metre in which each line has five stressed syllables (/) alternating with five unstressed syllables (×):

> × / × / × / × / × /
> You common cry of curs, whose breath I hate

At school, Shakespeare had learned the technical definition of iambic pentameter. In Greek 'penta' means five, and 'iamb' means a 'foot' of two syllables, the first unstressed, the second stressed, as in 'alas' pronounced aLAS. Shakespeare practised writing in that metre, and his early plays, such as *Titus Andronicus* or *Richard III*, are very regular in rhythm (often expressed as de-DUM de-DUM de-DUM de-DUM de-DUM), and with each line 'end-stopped' (making sense on its own).

By the time he came to write *Coriolanus* (around 1608), Shakespeare used great variation in his verse. Very few lines are completely 'regular' (five 'beats' in order). He adds extra syllables and varies the rhythm. Many lines are not 'end-stopped', the sense running over into the following line (*enjambement*). Many lines are 'shared', as a speaker ends a speech part way through a line and the line is completed by the next speaker. Some critics argue such sharing creates tension and interpersonal conflicts, others that it conveys a sense of genuine dialogue, with each speaker listening closely to what the other says, and replying.

Critical approaches

Traditional criticism

Coriolanus is the last tragedy Shakespeare wrote (around 1608), and it has always attracted less critical attention and acclaim than *Macbeth*, *King Lear*, *Othello* and *Hamlet*. The leading eighteenth-century critic Doctor Samuel Johnson (1765) found it 'one of the most amusing' of Shakespeare's plays ('amusing' in the sense of 'engaging the interest'), but considered:

> There is, perhaps, too much bustle in the first act, and too little in the last.

Criticism has traditionally employed two interrelated approaches to discuss the play: through character and through politics. For the Romantic critics in the first half of the nineteenth century (as for most later critics) the character of the 'hero', Coriolanus, was inexorably bound up with the political concerns and perspectives of the play. For William Hazlitt (1817) the play was 'a store-house of political commonplaces':

> The arguments for and against aristocracy or democracy, on the privileges of the few and the claims of the many, on liberty and slavery, power and the abuse of it, peace and war, are here very ably handled, with the spirit of a poet and the acuteness of a philosopher.

Like so many later critics, Hazlitt thought he could detect Shakespeare's own political leanings in the play (contempt for 'the rabble'). Here, Hazlitt differs from his fellow Romantic, Samuel Taylor Coleridge (1818), who stressed Shakespeare's 'wonderful philosophic impartiality', in that all characters, friends and enemies, expressed their views of Coriolanus, with 'the reader left to draw the whole'. In contrast, Hazlitt makes a bleak judgement on 'the logic of the imagination and the passions' of the play:

> The whole dramatic moral of *Coriolanus* is that those who have
> little shall have less, and that those who have much shall take
> all that others have left. The people are poor: therefore they
> ought to be starved. They are slaves: therefore they ought to be
> beaten. They work hard; therefore they ought to be treated like
> beasts of burden. They are ignorant; therefore they ought not
> to be allowed to feel that they want food, or clothing, or rest,
> that they are enslaved, oppressed and miserable.

Although nineteenth-century critics continued to discuss both politics and character, the latter usually became the dominant focus. Edward Dowden (1875) declared, 'The subject of *Coriolanus* is the ruin of a noble life through the sin of pride.' A C Swinburne (1880) sniffily dismissed the time 'spent if not wasted by able and even by eminent men on examination of *Coriolanus* with regard to its political aspect or bearing upon social questions'. For Swinburne:

> It is from first to last, for all its turmoil of battle and clamour of
> contentious factions, rather a private and domestic rather than
> a public or historical tragedy . . . The subject of the whole play
> is not the exile's revolt, the rebel's repentance, or the traitor's
> reward, but above all it is the son's tragedy.

The critic with whom the expression 'character study' is most associated is A C Bradley. Around 100 years ago, Bradley delivered a course of lectures at Oxford University which were published in 1904 as *Shakespearean Tragedy*. The book is centrally concerned with *Hamlet, Macbeth, Othello* and *King Lear*, and is still in print and widely read. In the book Bradley makes only a few brief references to *Coriolanus*, largely to the effect that certain passages bring the reader close to Shakespeare's mind. Bradley made a much more sustained critical analysis of the play eight years later in an essay significantly titled 'Character and the imaginative appeal of tragedy in *Coriolanus*'.

Bradley's assessment of the play makes depressing reading: 'scarcely popular', 'seldom acted', the tragedy 'least read' (after *Timon of Athens*). Bradley accuses Shakespeare of 'slackness' in some parts of the play, and regrets its 'obscurities of language'. In this, Bradley reflects much nineteenth- and early twentieth-century criticism, which was concerned to demonstrate that *Coriolanus* is inferior to

Shakespeare's other major tragedies. Bradley stresses how, unlike those tragedies, *Coriolanus* has no natural or supernatural element, but is intensely secular and public. But Bradley's prime concern is not with politics but with character, and he talks of the characters in the play as if they were real human beings of his time, experiencing familiar human emotions and thoughts. He identifies the desires and motives which give characters their particular personalities, and which evoke feelings of admiration or disapproval in the audience. For example, the plebeians are 'fundamentally good-natured, like the Englishmen they are, and have a humorous consciousness of their own weakness'.

Bradley regrets that Coriolanus, at moments of great passion, is not a great poet like Hamlet or other tragic heroes. He is 'very eloquent, but his only free eloquence is that of vituperation and scorn'. Nonetheless, in his greeting of Valeria in Act 5 Scene 3 lines 64–7 Bradley finds that 'in his huge violent heart there was a store, not only of tender affection, but of delicate and chivalrous poetry'. And Bradley's judgement on the play's hero is fundamentally favourable:

> He is altogether too simple and too ignorant of himself.
> Though he is the proudest man in Shakespeare he seems
> unaware of his pride, and is hurt when his mother mentions it.
> It does not prevent him from being genuinely modest . . .
> There is a greatness in all this that makes us exult.

Bradley's form of criticism reflects previous approaches to the play, and has strongly influenced critical approaches right up to the present. But his character approach has been much criticised, particularly for its neglect of the Elizabethan and Jacobean contexts of the play's creation: the cultural and intellectual assumptions of the time, stage conditions, and poetic and dramatic conventions.

The most frequent objection to Bradley is his treatment of characters as real people. But although Bradley has fallen from critical favour, his influence is still evident. Even modern criticism, whilst uneasy about discussing characters in this way, preferring to see them as fictional creations in a stage drama, finds it difficult to avoid writing about characters as if they were living people, and making moral judgements on them. Coriolanus and Volumnia have a presence that seems to demand a character approach.

However, it would be inappropriate to think of traditional criticism as concerned solely with character. All kinds of different approaches exist within it. For example T S Eliot (1919) judged the play 'Shakespeare's most assured artistic success', and other critics have attempted to reassess its genre (i.e. other than 'tragedy'). O J Campbell deemed it a 'tragical satire', mocking and derisive throughout. Kenneth Burke compared it to a Greek satyr-play: a 'grotesque' tragedy in which Coriolanus is a sacrificial victim in a ritual of purgation shared by the audience.

Other critics, whilst drawing attention to social aspects of the play, continue to demonstrate how character and society are inexorably bound up together in the play. Derek Traversi sees Coriolanus as an 'iron, mechanical warrior' and the play's key problem as 'a failure in sensitivity, a failure in living; and it represents a failure on the part of a whole society'. For L C Knights, Coriolanus demonstrates 'defective humanity', marked by lack of 'maturity' caused by Volumnia's 'taboo on tenderness'. Knights' judgement had been earlier expressed by Granville-Barker ('incorrigible boy') and more sharply by John Palmer in his *Political Characters of Shakespeare* (1945). Palmer claimed that *Coriolanus* 'is not the dramatisation of a political thesis . . . Shakespeare is intent on persons, not on public affairs'. Palmer's view of Coriolanus is:

> essentially the splendid oaf who has never come to maturity
> . . . It is this, in fact, that makes his conduct, which would be
> intolerable in a responsible adult, so far acceptable as to
> qualify him for the part of a tragic hero.

Wyndham Lewis (1966) is even more critical as he places Coriolanus both in Shakespeare's time and his own:

> Coriolanus is the demented 'aristocrat', the incarnation of
> violent snobbery . . . It is an astonishingly close picture of a
> particularly cheerless and unattractive snob, such as must have
> pullulated in the court of Elizabeth, and such as the English
> public-school and university system has produced ever since.

Caroline Spurgeon opened up a further critical perspective on *Coriolanus*: the study of its imagery. In *Shakespeare's Imagery and What it Tells Us*, Spurgeon identifies patterns of imagery in each of Shakespeare's plays. She finds that the dominant images of *Coriolanus* arise out of the theme of the body and sickness (see page 88 for examples), but she finds them 'very obvious, and rather laboured and overworked'. W H Clemen also finds the imagery 'obvious', but identifies it quite differently from Spurgeon. For Clemen the dominant imagery of the play is that which expresses the contrast between the plebeians (dogs, cats, curs, minnows, etc.) and Coriolanus (dragon, eagle, tiger, flower of warriors, the rock, a thing of blood, etc.).

The weakness of both Spurgeon's and Clemen's studies is that both claim that the imagery gives direct access to Shakespeare's own thoughts, feelings, nature and experience. Clemen, for example, claims that the imagery of *Coriolanus* reveals 'Shakespeare's intense dislike of the masses, of the never-to-be-trusted rabble', and his 'admiration for great and heroic men'. A much more critically aware and wide-ranging study of the play's imagery is that of Maurice Charney, who examines how the imagery relates to the dramatic context of the play, and gives due weight to images of acting and isolation.

G Wilson Knight (1951) finds imagery of violence, constriction and hardness in the play, with war and love in opposition: war is life-denying, love is life-giving. Knight expresses his view of *Coriolanus* in his typically cosmic imagery:

> He is a thing complete, a rounded perfection. We can no more blame him for his ruthless valour than we blame the hurtling spear for finding its mark. And yet Coriolanus has no mark: that is his tragedy . . . His wars are not for Rome: they are an end in themselves . . . So he whirls about like a planet in the dark chaos of pride, pursuing his self-bound orbit: a blind, mechanic, metallic thing of pride and pride's destiny.

Modern criticism

Throughout the second half of the twentieth century and in the twenty-first, critical approaches to Shakespeare have radically challenged the style and assumptions of the traditional approaches described above. New critical approaches argue that traditional interpretations, often heavily focused on character, are individualistic and misleading. The traditional concentration on personal feelings ignores society and history, and so divorces literary, dramatic and aesthetic matters from their social context. Further, their detachment from the real world makes them elitist, sexist and unpolitical.

Modern critical perspectives therefore shift the focus from individuals to how social conditions (of the world of the play, of Shakespeare's England) are reflected in characters' relationships, language and behaviour. Modern criticism also concerns itself with how changing social assumptions at different periods of time have affected interpretations of the play.

What follows explores how modern critical approaches to Shakespeare have been used to address *Coriolanus*. Like traditional criticism, contemporary perspectives include many different approaches but share common features. Modern criticism:

- is sceptical of 'character' approaches (but often uses them);
- concentrates on political, social and economic factors (arguing that these factors determine Shakespeare's creativity and audiences' and critics' interpretations);
- identifies contradictions, fragmentation and disunity in the plays;
- questions the possibility of 'happy' or 'hopeful' endings, preferring ambiguous, unsettling or sombre endings;
- produces readings that are subversive of existing social structures;
- identifies how the plays express the interests of dominant groups, particularly rich and powerful males;
- insists that 'theory' (psychological, social, etc.) is essential to produce valid readings;
- often expresses its commitment (for example, to feminism, or equality, or anti-colonialism, or political change);
- argues all readings are political or ideological readings (and that traditional criticism falsely claims to be objective);
- argues that traditional approaches have always interpreted Shakespeare conservatively, in ways that confirm and maintain the interests of the elite or dominant class.

The following discussion is organised under headings which represent major contemporary critical perspectives on *Coriolanus* (political, feminist, performance, psychoanalytic and postmodern).

But it is vital to appreciate that there is often overlap between the categories, and that to pigeonhole any example of criticism too precisely is to reduce its value and application. Any single critical essay may have a dominant focus, but it usually takes account of other approaches.

Political criticism

'Political criticism' is a convenient label for approaches concerned with power and social structure: in the world of the play, in Shakespeare's time and in our own. As noted in the 'Traditional criticism' section above, there is a long history of approaching the play through its politics, because politics and character are so intertwined. The very nature of the play (or perhaps, less contentiously, what happens in the play) makes it virtually impossible for any critic not to comment on the class conflict between plebeians and patricians (but often without using such a term as 'class conflict').

Kenneth Burke (1977), for example, holds that Shakespeare saw an analogy between the dispossessed poor of his own day and the Roman plebeians. He argues that in *Coriolanus* Shakespeare thus dramatises Jacobean social concerns. In a different, but still 'political' approach, D J Enright (1954) considered the play rather like an 'intellectual debate', and 'unusually narrow for Shakespeare'. In that narrow focus, Rome's inhabitants:

> form parties rather than relationships. Their first question is
> 'What is in it for us?' . . . its final impression of aridness and
> waste might well be considered a warning against that
> petrification of humanity which occurs when people think only
> in terms of parties and movements and manifestoes

A P Rossiter (1961) in his influential *Angel with Horns* has a chapter on *Coriolanus* in which he reads the play as a tragedy. But it is a tragedy about the historical process, like Shakespeare's history plays in which the protagonist is not an individual, but the State. For Rossiter, '*Coriolanus* is about power: about State, or the State; about order in society and the forces of disorder' which threaten that integrity. But Rossiter conveys a subtle understanding of the politics of *Coriolanus*:

By 'political' I do not mean the class-war, nor even narrowly the Tudor system of God-ordained order. I mean *Coriolanus* plays on political feeling: the capacity to be not only intellectually, but emotionally and purposively, engaged by the management of public affairs; the businesses of men in (ordered) communities; the contrivance or maintenance of agreement; the establishment of a will-in-common . . .

Rossiter finds the 'excitement' of the play in 'all that unstable, shifting, trustless, feckless, foolish–shrewd, canny, short-sighted, self-seeking, high-minded, confused, confusing matter which makes up a State's state of mind'. In Rossiter's liberal-humanist approach, he thus judges *Coriolanus* as 'the last and greatest of (Shakespeare's) histories. It is Shakespeare's only great political play'.

A well-known critic who is often called in support of political interpretations of Shakespeare's plays is the Polish scholar Jan Kott. Kott fought with the Polish army and underground movement against the Nazis in the Second World War (1939–45), and had direct experience of the suffering and terror caused by Stalinist repression in Poland in the years after the war. His book, *Shakespeare Our Contemporary*, saw parallels between the violence and cruelty of the modern world and the worlds of tyranny and despair that Shakespeare depicted in his tragedies. His discussion of *Coriolanus* is similarly concerned to show how it reflects modern political cynicism, violence, class conflict and social breakdown. As such, it fits with Kott's pessimistic vision of the absurd and purposeless nature of history.

Kott interprets the first half of the play as having 'a republican moral' (the banishment of a would-be dictator). He detects three conceptions of society in the play: the plebeians', expressing egalitarianism; Coriolanus', expressing hierarchy; and Menenius' fable of the belly, expressing solidarity. All three, Kott claims, are contradicted in the play: the plebeians are cowardly looters, hierarchy exacts cruel punishments of the underclass or defeated, and solidarity of classes or individuals is denied by the play's events. 'History', claims Kott, has caught Coriolanus, 'and driven him into a blind alley; has made a double traitor of him.' For Kott the play offers no solutions to the contradictions of history:

The world contradicts the laws of nature. But in the name of the same laws Coriolanus has been condemned by his mother, wife and son. He has to condemn himself. Coriolanus feels he has been caught, fallen into a trap set for him by the ruthless and all too real world . . . he wanted to play the role of an avenging deity, while in the scenario of history he was given only the role of a traitor.

Victor Kiernan's 1996 Marxist study of Shakespeare's plays gives a historically located account of *Coriolanus* as a criticism of the values, role models and social organisations that give rise to a character like its warrior-hero:

Shakespeare is growing tired of great men, however, and one like Coriolanus must necessarily be self-destructive, because he cannot really be a man. He is an embodiment of aristocratic arrogance, almost a mechanical contrivance . . . Coriolanus is the champion of power, or might is right . . . he resembles the bulk of the European nobility in Shakespeare's time in being fit for nothing except fighting . . . with Coriolanus we are back in a rude age of warfare, far removed from the Renaissance ideal of soldier, courtier, scholar, all in one . . . The play is a striking exposition of how aggressive nationalism and acute social division not only may, but must, go together; the former not only as a means of hoodwinking the poor, but as a way for the rulers to throw dust in their own eyes and have a good conscience to bolster them . . . The play is in many ways . . . a study of aristocratic flattery and cajoling of the people for the purpose of duping them . . . Shakespeare takes leave of a republic deadlocked, with no way out except perpetual war and conquest.

Feminist criticism

Feminism aims to achieve rights and equality for women in social, political and economic life. It challenges sexism: those beliefs and practices which result in the degradation, oppression and subordination of women. Feminist critics therefore reject 'male ownership' of criticism in which men determined what questions were to be asked of a play, and which answers were acceptable. They argue that male criticism often neglects, represses or misrepresents and stereotypes female experience, or distorts women's points of view.

Feminists often approach a Shakespeare play using the notion of patriarchy: male domination of women. Feminists point to the fact that throughout history power has been in the hands of men, both in society and in the family. Feminist criticism therefore makes much of the fact that Rome is a male-dominated society that values bravery in war as its prime virtue. Manhood is the desired goal of all males, and women are required to bear and bring up male children to achieve the masculinity that Rome prizes. In that process Volumnia is fully complicit, eagerly framing her son from his earliest years to the murderous masculinity of his warrior status. Rome may be ruled by males, but Volumnia is the most willing agent of its values. In contrast, Virgilia recoils from what that status involves: wounds, blood, suffering. Her response registers the feminine values that seem so marginalised in the play.

Volumnia subverts Elizabethan and Jacobean negative stereotypes of women as weak, submissive and pliable. And paradoxically, in the overwhelmingly male world of Rome, it is the women who exercise the most important power at the play's end. It is their pleading, their presence, even their silence, that saves Rome from destruction, and at the same time seals Coriolanus' fate. And yet, in the play, characters dismiss feminine qualities as inferior. Coriolanus recoils from the suggestion he should play a part to deceive the plebeians into giving him their voices, equating it with 'some harlot's spirit'.

Probably the best-known feminist critic of *Coriolanus* is Coppelia Kahn. Her book, *Roman Shakespeare: Warriors, Wounds, and Women*, claims that Shakespeare's Roman plays 'articulate a critique of the ideology of gender'. She makes the point that gender (masculinity, femininity) is constructed, not something given at birth, and that in his Roman plays Shakespeare exposes how that construction takes place. The relevance of Kahn's subtitle (*Warriors, Wounds, and Women*) to *Coriolanus* is evident (and Kahn claims these three terms constitute 'Shakespeare's problematic of manly virtue'). 'Warriors' stresses that Coriolanus seeks to emulate the great war heroes of the past. 'Wounds' are the physical, visible attributes of Roman virtue, and yet at the same time they signify vulnerability associated with women.

'Women' are basic to the construction of males as Romans. Using these concepts, Kahn claims that:

> In his most unsparing critique of manly virtue, Shakespeare shows in Volumnia the awesome power of the mother, once she is complicit with the ideology of *virtus*, to mould her son into a sword.

Kahn points out that Shakespeare places Volumnia at the centre of the play, and makes her 'pertinent at every moment to the tragic action'. Her authority derives from being a mother and from identifying with the 'masculinist, military ideology of Rome'. Her story of how she brought up her son ('To a cruel war I sent him') shows both her affection and how she transcended that affection. In Volumnia's control of Coriolanus' development, Kahn sees how 'she exercises a uniquely maternal power that eludes patriarchal control over women'. Kahn's conclusion is a powerful testament to maternal power:

> *Coriolanus* ends ironically, with Volumnia hailed as 'the life of Rome' while her son, unknown to the Romans, is hacked to death by the Volsces. In every sense, she prevails: over his desire for revenge, his rigidly consistent masculinity and the impotent patricians. Yet it was her maternal power, assigned her by the state, that locked her son into the fatal contradiction of his manhood and turned him into an enemy of the state. In yet another of several prominent reversals, the mother who lives only through her son survives while he is sacrificed so that she and the city with which she is identified may live.

Feminist readings, like all critical interpretations, raise the question of whether they are what Shakespeare intended. Whilst most critics today argue that Shakespeare's intentions can never be known, a distinctive feature of feminist criticism is to suggest that *Coriolanus* does expose the aridity and death-directed masculine values of Rome and its warrior-hero.

Performance criticism

Performance criticism fully acknowledges that *Coriolanus* is a play: a script to be performed by actors to an audience. It examines all aspects of the play in performance: its staging in the theatre or on video.

Performance criticism focuses on Shakespeare's stagecraft and the semiotics (signs: words, costumes, gestures, etc.) of theatre, together with the 'afterlife' of the play (what happened to *Coriolanus* after Shakespeare wrote it). That involves scrutiny of how productions at different periods have presented the play. As such, performance criticism appraises how the text has been cut, added to, rewritten and rearranged to present a version felt appropriate to the times.

Shakespeare probably wrote *Coriolanus* around 1608, but there is no record of a production in his lifetime. The play appeared in print for the first time in 1623 in the First Folio (see page 74), but for the next 200 years very free adaptations were much more popular than Shakespeare's original. The adaptations were often written in response to threats to civil order. For example, versions of the play proved popular after the 1715 and 1745 Jacobite rebellions. In both rebellions, an army invaded England in an unsuccessful attempt to overthrow the Hanoverian monarchy and place an exile from the house of Stuart on the throne.

The titles of the adaptations provide clues to their approach. *The Invader of His Country or The Fatal Resentment* (1720), a rewriting by John Dennis, was prompted by the 1715 rebellion. A version by James Thompson, reacting to the 1745 rebellion, became *Coriolanus: or The Roman Matron* (1752). It was performed with almost 200 actors on stage. In 1782 Nahum Tate (who rewrote *King Lear* with a happy ending) staged his version: *The Ingratitude of a Commonwealth, or the Fall of Coriolanus*. In Tate's revision, Menenius and young Martius are murdered, Valeria becomes a chatterbox and flirt, Aufidius dies, and Coriolanus is reunited with his family.

Nineteenth-century productions of the play were popular in the republican USA. In England, performances were much concerned with spectacle. Grand processions and battle scenes were staged, and productions attempted to create the 'authentic' architecture of ancient Rome on stage. One production included a giant lighthouse at Antium in its scenery.

Adaptations continued in the twentieth century. The English playwright John Osborne rewrote the play as *A Place Calling Itself Rome*. Osborne set the play in 1970s Britain, torn by labour disputes and demonstrations. The German playwright and director, Berthold Brecht, a committed communist, prepared a left-wing adaptation of the play to criticise militarism. His version plays down Coriolanus' nobility and emphasises the strength and solidarity of the people under the tribunes. In the production performed after Brecht's death, the plebeians refused to fight until they were given corn, and the play ended with the tribunes curtly dismissing a plea that Coriolanus' memory should be honoured.

But throughout the twentieth century and into the twenty-first Shakespeare's own play became increasingly popular around the world. Modern productions have usually sought parallels with the political and social preoccupations of their time. The dramatic appeal of the play is evident. The play's concern with leadership and the right to rule, enables productions to express current preoccupations about social and political issues. Some productions explored the relationship of democratic, military and fascist values. Others have been more concerned with gender issues and the psychological relationships of mother and son, or Coriolanus and Aufidius. For example, one production, influenced by Freudian theory, portrayed a homoerotic relationship between the two men.

The power of *Coriolanus* to express current political anxieties is evident. In Paris in 1933 there were riots at every performance of the play. Right-wing factions hailed Coriolanus as a perfect hero who had been wrongly victimised. The disturbances led to the police closing down the production. The government dismissed the theatre's director and replaced him with a former chief of police. The play was popular in Communist states, and was used to explore relations between individual and society. A production in Moscow in 1934 portrayed Coriolanus as a self-seeking leader who betrayed his people.

With Britain moving towards war with Nazi Germany, a 1938 London Old Vic production presented an anti-fascist interpretation. But in Nazi Germany in the 1930s the play became a school text with an anti-democratic message. Students were urged to think of Hitler as being like Coriolanus, a strong leader unjustly treated. After the war the occupying American forces banned performances of *Coriolanus* in their sector of Germany from 1945 to 1953.

The theatrical potential of Shakespeare's stagecraft ensures the play's attractiveness to actors and audiences. The tight focus on Coriolanus heightens dramatic tension, and there are great opportunities for theatrical spectacle in staging crowd protests, triumphal processions and battle scenes with all the noise of drums and trumpets. One production introduced battering rams to assault the gates of Corioles; another used siege ladders. Modern performances have staged the play in all kinds of periods and costumes: Napoleonic, nineteenth-century Germany, pre-Civil War America, Mussolini's Italy of the 1930s, Al Capone's Chicago, Central America with Sandanista guerillas, Vietnam, the Solidarity movement in Poland and the 1991 Desert Storm offensive in Kuwait. Battle scenes have been played in slow motion, and in Japanese martial arts style (the 2002–3 Royal Shakespeare Company production presented Coriolanus as a blood-soaked samurai warrior). Coriolanus has been variously depicted as Napoleon, Mussolini, General George Patten (a World War Two hero), a Victorian soldier. In 1959 Laurence Olivier played Coriolanus as a Roman *Junker*, resembling a stiff-necked Prussian general.

Psychoanalytic criticism

In the twentieth century, psychoanalysis became a major influence on the understanding and interpretation of human behaviour. The founder of psychoanalysis, Sigmund Freud, explained personality as the result of unconscious and irrational desires, repressed memories or wishes, sexuality, fantasy, anxiety and conflict. Freud's theories have had a strong influence on criticism and stagings of Shakespeare's plays, most famously on *Hamlet* in the well-known claim that Hamlet suffers from an Oedipus complex.

Coriolanus, and its fraught family relationships, has prompted much attention from critics who adopt a psychoanalytic approach to Shakespeare's plays. Norman Holland, in *Psychoanalysis and Shakespeare*, asserts that psychoanalysts 'consider *Coriolanus*, not unreasonably, another oedipal play, although one stressing the relationship of mother to son rather than the rivalry of father and son'. Most psychoanalytic readings flow from interpretations of Volumnia's tale of Coriolanus' loveless childhood and his subsequent infantile relationship with his mother, which fuels Coriolanus' anxieties about autonomy. Here is a selection of such interpretations:

- Coriolanus' childhood frustrations cause his aggression.
- Coriolanus' 'tragic flaw' is tremendous power coupled with a fatal dependency on his mother.
- Coriolanus' soldierly violence is displaced rage against his mother; his attack on Rome represents a sadistic but unsuccessful attack on his mother.

- Coriolanus has two conflicting needs: achievement (to establish independence from his mother), and dependence (to receive at her breast love, praise and milk of human kindness).
- Volumnia has been variously interpreted as castrator, as living out her fantasies of manhood through her son, and as displaying seeming affection and pride in her son which masks her underlying hatred.

Probably the best known psychoanalytic approach to the play is that of Janet Adelman (1992). She sees eating as the central image of the play, with Volumnia as a non-nurturant mother who has not fed her children. Adelman sees Volumnia's attitude towards food 'nicely summed up' in her rejection of Menenius' invitation to dinner: 'Anger's my meat. I sup upon myself, / And so shall starve with feeding.' But even more crucial to Adelman is Volumnia's 'glee' at the thought of Coriolanus' wounds:

> The breasts of Hecuba,
> When she did suckle Hector, looked not lovelier
> Than Hector's forehead when it spit forth blood
> At Grecian sword, contemning.   *(Act 1 Scene 3, lines 35–8)*

Adelman claims the lines show 'Blood is more beautiful than milk, the wound than the breast, warfare than peaceful feeding . . . Hector doesn't stand a chance in Volumnia's imagination: he is transformed immediately from infantile feeding mouth to bleeding wound.' In Adelman's view, that 'does not bode well for Coriolanus'.

Such interpretations reveal that psychoanalytic approaches are a specialised type of character criticism (like psychiatric case histories). They also demonstrate the obvious weaknesses in applying psychoanalytic theories to *Coriolanus*. They cannot be proved or disproved, and they are highly speculative. But the play's evident interest in troubled mother–son relationships explains why many critics are confident in employing psychoanalytic concepts in their interpretations.

Postmodern criticism

Postmodern criticism (sometimes called 'deconstruction' or 'post-structuralism') is often difficult to understand because it is not centrally concerned with consistency or reasoned argument. It does not accept that one section of the story is necessarily connected to what follows, or that characters relate to each other in meaningful ways. The approach therefore has obvious drawbacks in providing a model for examination students who are expected to display reasoned, coherent argument, and respect for the evidence of the text.

Postmodern approaches to *Coriolanus* are most clearly seen in stage productions. There, you could think of it as simply 'a mixture of styles'. The label 'postmodern' is applied to productions which self-consciously show little regard for consistency in character, or for coherence in telling the story. Characters are dressed in costumes from very different historical periods.

Postmodern criticism most typically revels in the cleverness of its own use of language, and accepts all kinds of anomalies and contradictions in a spirit of playfulness or 'carnival'. It abandons any notion of the organic unity of the play, and rejects the assumption that a Shakespeare play possesses clear patterns or themes. Some postmodern critics even deny the possibility of finding meaning in language. They claim that words simply refer to other words, and so any interpretation is endlessly delayed (or 'deferred', as the deconstructionists say).

Coriolanus has attracted little sustained postmodern criticism. That is probably because the comparatively narrow focus of the play, its clear storyline and its evident concern with politics and character, resists such 'playful' approaches. As the following example from Terry Eagleton (1986) shows, character and political concerns dominate over a postmodern desire to reduce Coriolanus to mere language ('a blank tautology'):

> Coriolanus, though literally a patrician, is perhaps Shakespeare's most developed study of a bourgeois individualist, . . . Coriolanus confers value and meaning on himself in fine disregard for social opinion . . . Coriolanus is nothing but his actions, a circular, blindly persistent process of self-definition. . . . he is exactly what he is, and so a sort of blank tautology.

Organising your responses

The purpose of this section is to help you improve your writing about *Coriolanus*. It offers practical guidance on two kinds of tasks: writing about an extract from the play and writing an essay. Whether you are answering an examination question, preparing coursework (term papers), or carrying out research into your own chosen topic, this section will help you organise and present your responses.

In all your writing, there are three vital things to remember:

- *Coriolanus* is a play. Although it is usually referred to as a 'text', *Coriolanus* is not a book, but a script intended to be acted on a stage. So your writing should demonstrate an awareness of the play in performance as theatre. That means you should always try to read the play with an 'inner eye', thinking about how it could look and sound on stage. The next best thing to seeing an actual production is to imagine yourself sitting in the audience, watching and listening to *Coriolanus* being performed. By doing so, you will be able to write effectively about Shakespeare's language and dramatic techniques.

- *Coriolanus* is not a presentation of 'reality'. It is a dramatic construct in which the playwright, through theatre, engages the emotions and intellect of the audience. The characters and story may persuade an audience to suspend its disbelief for several hours. The audience may identify with the characters, be deeply moved by them, and may think of them as if they are living human beings. However, when you write, a major part of your task is to show how Shakespeare achieves his dramatic effects that so engage the audience. Through discussion of his handling of language, character and plot, your writing should reveal how Shakespeare uses themes and ideas, attitudes and values, to give insight into crucial social, moral and political dilemmas of his time – and yours.

- How Shakespeare learned his craft. As a schoolboy, and in his early years as a dramatist, Shakespeare used all kinds of models or frameworks to guide his writing. But he quickly learned how to vary and adapt the models to his own dramatic purposes. This section offers frameworks that you can use to structure your writing. As you use them, follow Shakespeare's example! Adapt them to suit your own writing style and needs.

Writing about an extract

It is an expected part of all Shakespeare study that you should be able to write well about an extract (sometimes called a 'passage') from the play. An extract is usually between 30 and 70 lines long, and you are invited to comment on it. The instructions vary. Sometimes the task is very briefly expressed:

- Write a detailed commentary on the following passage.
- Write about the effect of the extract on your own thoughts and feelings.

At other times a particular focus is specified for your writing:

- With close reference to the language and imagery of the passage, show in what ways it helps to establish important issues in the play.
- Analyse the style and structure of the extract, showing what it contributes to your appreciation of the play's major concerns.

In writing your response, you must of course take account of the precise wording of the task, and ensure you concentrate on each particular point specified. But however the invitation to write about an extract is expressed, it requires you to comment in detail on the language. You should identify and evaluate how the language reveals character, contributes to plot development, offers opportunities for dramatic effect, and embodies crucial concerns of the play as a whole. These 'crucial concerns' are also referred to as the 'themes', or 'issues', or 'preoccupations' of the play.

The following framework is a guide to how you can write a detailed commentary on an extract. Writing a paragraph or more on each item will help you bring out the meaning and significance of the extract, and show how Shakespeare achieves his effects.

Although the framework identifies ten paragraphs, you may of course choose to write more than one paragraph under any heading.

Paragraph 1: Locate the extract in the play and say who is on stage.
Paragraph 2: State what the extract is about and identify its structure.
Paragraph 3: Identify the mood or atmosphere of the extract.

Paragraphs 4–8:
   Diction (vocabulary)
   Imagery
   Antithesis
   Repetition
   Lists

These paragraphs analyse how Shakespeare achieves his effects. They concentrate on the language of the extract, showing the dramatic effect of each item, and how the language expresses crucial concerns of the play.

Paragraph 9: Staging opportunities
Paragraph 10: Conclusion

The analysis and examples of different types of language use in this Guide (imagery, antithesis etc., see pages 85–93) will help you in constructing your own response. The following example uses the framework to show how the paragraphs making up the essay might be written. The framework headings (in bold) would not of course appear in your essay. They are presented only to help you see how the framework is used. The extract is from Act 5 Scene 6, lines 71–132 (you will also find it helpful to read how the passage is discussed in the commentary, pages 70–2).

Extract

Enter CORIOLANUS *marching with drum and colours, the* COMMONERS
    being with him

CORIOLANUS Hail, lords! I am returned your soldier,   *1*
    No more infected with my country's love
    Than when I parted hence, but still subsisting
    Under your great command. You are to know
    That prosperously I have attempted and   *5*
    With bloody passage led your wars even to
    The gates of Rome. Our spoils we have brought home
    Doth more than counterpoise a full third part
    The charges of the action. We have made peace
    With no less honour to the Antiates   *10*
    Than shame to th'Romans. And we here deliver,
    Subscribed by th'consuls and patricians,

Together with the seal o'th'senate, what
We have compounded on.

[*He offers a document*]

AUFIDIUS   Read it not, noble lords,
But tell the traitor in the highest degree   15
He hath abused your powers.

CORIOLANUS 'Traitor'? How now?

AUFIDIUS Ay, traitor, Martius.

CORIOLANUS 'Martius'?

AUFIDIUS Ay, Martius, Caius Martius. Dost thou think   20
I'll grace thee with that robbery, thy stol'n name
Coriolanus, in Corioles? –
You lords and heads o'th'state, perfidiously
He has betrayed your business and given up,
For certain drops of salt, your city Rome –   25
I say 'your city' – to his wife and mother,
Breaking his oath and resolution like
A twist of rotten silk, never admitting
Counsel o'th'war. But at his nurse's tears
He whined and roared away your victory,   30
That pages blushed at him and men of heart
Looked wondering each at others.

CORIOLANUS   Hear'st thou, Mars?

AUFIDIUS Name not the god, thou boy of tears.

CORIOLANUS   Ha?

AUFIDIUS No more.

CORIOLANUS Measureless liar, thou hast made my heart   35
Too great for what contains it. 'Boy'? O slave! –
Pardon me, lords, 'tis the first time that ever
I was forced to scold. Your judgements, my grave lords,
Must give this cur the lie; and his own notion –
Who wears my stripes impressed upon him, that   40
Must bear my beating to his grave – shall join
To thrust the lie unto him.

FIRST LORD Peace, both, and hear me speak.

CORIOLANUS Cut me to pieces, Volsces. Men and lads,
Stain all your edges on me. 'Boy'! False hound,   45
If you have writ your annals true, 'tis there
That, like an eagle in a dovecote, I

Fluttered your Volscians in Corioles.
Alone I did it. 'Boy'!

AUFIDIUS   Why, noble lords,
Will you be put in mind of his blind fortune,   50
Which was your shame, by this unholy braggart,
'Fore your own eyes and ears?

ALL CONSPIRATORS   Let him die for't.

ALL PEOPLE Tear him to pieces! Do it presently! He killed my son!
My daughter! He killed my cousin Marcus! He killed my father!

SECOND LORD Peace, ho! No outrage. Peace!   55
The man is noble, and his fame folds in
This orb o'th'earth. His last offences to us
Shall have judicious hearing. Stand, Aufidius,
And trouble not the peace.

CORIOLANUS   O that I had him,
With six Aufidiuses, or more, his tribe,   60
To use my lawful sword!

AUFIDIUS   Insolent villain!

ALL CONSPIRATORS Kill, kill, kill, kill, kill him!

The Conspirators draw their swords, and kill Martius, who falls;
Aufidius stands on him

Paragraph 1: Locate the extract in the play and say who is on stage.
It is the final scene of the play. Coriolanus, moved by the entreaty of
his mother, Volumnia, has abandoned his desire for revenge on
Rome. He has withdrawn his Volsce army, made a peace treaty with
the Romans, and now returns to Corioles to present the treaty to the
Volsce lords. But Aufidius and his conspirators are present, planning
to accuse Coriolanus of treason and kill him.

Paragraph 2: State what the extract is about and identify its structure.
(Begin with one or two sentences identifying what the extract is about,
followed by several sentences briefly identifying its structure – that is,
the unfolding events and the different sections of the extract.)

The extract dramatises how Aufidius puts into action his plan to
kill Coriolanus. Coriolanus enters in military pomp, accompanied by
enthusiastically supportive Volsce plebeians. He tells of a successful
outcome to his campaign against Rome, and tries to present the peace

treaty to the Volsce lords. But Aufidius accuses him of treason, insults him as 'Martius', accuses him of yielding to the tears of women and sparing Rome, and insultingly calls him 'boy'. Coriolanus is enraged at the insults, and despite the Volsce lords' attempts to calm the situation, arrogantly mocks Aufidius and the Volsces, taunting them with the fact that he conquered Corioles single-handed. Reminded of Coriolanus' butchery of their relatives, the Volsce plebeians turn against Coriolanus, and he is killed by Aufidius' conspirators.

Paragraph 3: Identify the mood or atmosphere of the extract.
There are distinct shifts of mood throughout the extract, as potential menace turns to bloody execution. It begins with Coriolanus' seemingly triumphal entry and his diplomatically expressed speech to the Volsce lords. Throughout this, the watching Aufidius and his conspirators create a mood of sinister anticipation. The atmosphere changes to one of direct hostility as Aufidius accuses and insults Coriolanus, who at first seems puzzled by what he hears. But as he grasps Aufidius' meaning, and is stung by the insulting 'boy', Coriolanus explodes to create a mood of anger, disdain and contempt. Aufidius and the conspirators inflame the Volsce plebeians to virulent condemnation, and Coriolanus, expressing implacable defiance, is bloodily killed. Aufidius creates a moment of humiliation by standing on Coriolanus' body.

Paragraph 4: Diction (vocabulary)
Coriolanus' opening speech seems out of character with his language in the rest of the play, sounding more like that of a politician than a proud, arrogant warrior. An expression like 'counterpoise a full third part' (exceeding by a third) is the sort of accountancy language alien to Coriolanus. Elsewhere, 'the Antiates' are the Volsces, 'compounded on' means 'agreed' and 'blind fortune' means 'mere good luck'. Both Aufidius and Coriolanus deliberately use words that they know will enrage the other. Aufidius uses 'Martius' (rather than Coriolanus), 'traitor', 'nurse's tears', 'whined and roared' and 'boy'. Coriolanus' insulting words include 'liar', 'slave', 'cur', 'stripes', 'false hound' and 'tribe'.

Paragraph 5: Imagery
Vivid images echo imagery and themes that run through the play.

Coriolanus declares he is not 'infected' by love for Rome, recalling past disease imagery. Aufidius' 'drops of salt' (tears), 'nurse's tears' (mother's weeping) and 'pages blushed' (boys were embarrassed) all insult Coriolanus' manhood and dependence on his mother, a constant preoccupation of the play. Comparing Coriolanus' oath-breaking to 'A twist of rotten silk' is an image that conveys the corruption of treachery. In response, Coriolanus contemptuously speaks of the 'stripes' (wounds) he has inflicted on Aufidius and mockingly invites the Volsces to turn their 'edges' (swords) on him. But the most striking image of the passage is the simile of Coriolanus' single-handed slaughter of the Volsces at Corioles, like an eagle loose in a dovecote, killing at will. It is a cruel picture of what the Roman 'valour' entails. And themes of nobility and renown underline the Volsce claim that Coriolanus' fame covers the whole word ('folds in / This orb o'th'earth').

Paragraph 6: Antithesis
The conflict that characterises the entire play (Volsces versus Romans, plebeians versus patricians, etc.) is further deepened by the antitheses in the passage. Coriolanus sets 'my country's love' against 'your great command' (Rome versus Antium) and 'honour' against 'shame'. Both oppose Rome to the Volsces. Aufidius insultingly sets 'grace' against 'stolen' and contrasts Coriolanus' infantile cowardice ('whined and roared') with the wonder of brave men ('men of heart'). He even more woundingly contrasts Coriolanus' appeal to 'Mars' (god of war) with 'boy of tears'. And Coriolanus' soaring image is itself an antithesis as the remorseless eagle causes havoc among the helpless doves.

Paragraph 7: Repetition
Clearly, the repetition of key words serves to heighten dramatic effect as they inflame Coriolanus: 'boy', 'traitor' and 'Martius'. But there are more subtle repetitions that achieve their own dramatic purposes. The measured rhythm of Coriolanus' first speech suggests it is a prepared political statement. Aufidius' use of 'your' constantly reminds the Volsce lords of how Coriolanus has treacherously given away what belongs to them: 'your powers', 'your business', 'your city Rome', 'your victory'. But the most striking repetition dramatically accompanies Coriolanus' fate: 'Kill, kill, kill, kill, kill him!'

Paragraph 8: Lists

Shakespeare's technique of piling item on item is most evident as the Volsce plebeians list their stored-up reasons for hatred of Coriolanus: 'He killed my son! My daughter!', etc. Their catalogue of grievance creates dramatic opportunities for creating an atmosphere of isolating Coriolanus among his enemies, and also serves to show yet again the play's portrayal of the fickleness of the plebeians, whether Roman or Volsce. Elsewhere Coriolanus' first speech can be seen as a carefully constructed sequence listing event after event: 'returned your soldier', 'led your wars', made a profit from 'Our spoils', 'made peace', 'here deliver'. And Aufidius' contemptuous report of Coriolanus' behaviour and boys' and men's reactions is an example of Shakespeare building a vividly effective sequence of condemnation: 'whined and roared', 'blushed' and 'wondering'.

Paragraph 9: Staging opportunities

The extract offers opportunities for thrilling theatrical presentation. Coriolanus' entry can be ceremoniously staged as a triumph, which can be sinisterly undermined as the audience watch the silent Aufidius and his conspirators waiting for their moment. Next, the confrontation as Aufidius accuses Coriolanus of treachery and cowardice offers multiple dramatic possibilities because the Volsce lords are as amazed as Coriolanus by the charges. Coriolanus' return to his usual arrogant, defiant and contemptuous style is the next intensely dramatic moment, and productions can be guided by his boast 'Alone I did it', to heighten the audience's sense that Coriolanus is totally isolated among his enemies. Finally, the staging of his death presents every production with a dramatic challenge, and it is worth recalling perhaps the most breathtaking death scene of all in which Laurence Olivier fell from a high platform and hung suspended by his ankles in a posture that echoed the humiliating display of the body of the Italian dictator, Mussolini, at the end of the 1939–45 war.

Paragraph 10: Conclusion

The extract, virtually at the end of the play, reminds the audience of many of the themes of the play: pride, valour (the chief Roman virtue), conflict, betrayal, the mother–son relationship, the fickleness of plebeians. All are concretely expressed in the language and action of the passage. And there is even a touch of humour in the passage as

Coriolanus, who has ranted and raged his way through so much of the play, asks for pardon as he declares ''tis the first time that ever / I was forced to scold'. It ironically recalls his dismissive 'mildly' as he went to face the tribunes and people in the marketplace.

Reminders

- The framework is only a guide. It helps you to structure your writing. Use the framework for practice on other extracts. Adapt as you feel appropriate. Make it your own.
- Structure your response in paragraphs. Each paragraph makes a particular point and helps build up your argument.
- Focus tightly on the language, especially vocabulary, imagery, antithesis, lists, repetitions.
- Remember that *Coriolanus* is a play, a drama intended for performance. The purpose of writing about an extract is to identify how Shakespeare creates dramatic effect. What techniques does he use?
- Try to imagine the action. Visualise the scene in your mind's eye. But remember there can be many valid ways of performing a scene. Offer alternatives. Justify your own preferences by reference to the language.
- Who is on stage? Imagine their interaction. How do 'silent characters' react to what's said?
- Look for the theatrical qualities of the extract. What guides for actors' movement and expressions are given in the language? Comment on any stage directions.
- How might the audience respond? In Jacobean times? Today? How might you respond as a member of the audience?
- How might the lines be spoken? What about tone, emphasis, pace, pauses? Identify shifting moods and registers. What are the characteristics of the verse or prose (see page 92)?
- What is the importance of the extract in the play as a whole? Justify its thematic significance.
- Are there 'key words'?
- How does the extract develop the plot, reveal character, deepen themes?
- Offer a variety of interpretations.

Writing an essay

As part of your study of *Coriolanus* you will be asked to write essays, either under examination conditions or for coursework (term papers). Examinations mean that you are under pressure of time, usually having around one hour to prepare and write each essay. Coursework means that you have much longer to think about and produce your essay. But whatever the type of essay, each will require you to develop an argument about a particular aspect of *Coriolanus*.

Before suggesting a strategy for your essay-writing, it is helpful to recall just what an essay is. Essay comes from the French *essai*: 'an attempt', or 'a trial'. It was originally used by the sixteenth-century French writer Montaigne (whose work Shakespeare certainly read). Montaigne used *essais* to attempt to find out what he thought about particular subjects, such as 'friendship', or 'cannibals' or 'education'. In each essay he used many practical examples to test his response to the topic.

The essays you write on *Coriolanus* similarly require that you set out your thoughts on a particular aspect of the play, using evidence from the text. The people who read your essays (examiners, teachers, lecturers) will have certain expectations of your writing. In each essay they will expect you to discuss and analyse a particular topic, using evidence from the play to develop an argument in an organised, coherent and persuasive way. Examiners look for, and reward, what they call 'an informed personal response'. This simply means that you show you have good knowledge of the play ('informed') and can use evidence from it to support and justify your own viewpoint ('personal').

You can write about *Coriolanus* from different points of view. As pages 98–109 show, you can approach the play from a number of critical perspectives (political, psychoanalytic, feminist, etc.). You can also set the play in its social, literary, political and other contexts, as shown in pages 74–84. You should write at different levels, moving beyond description to analysis and evaluation. Simply telling the story or describing characters is not as effective as analysing how events or characters embody wider concerns of the play, its themes, issues and preoccupations. In your writing, always give practical examples (quotations, actions) which illustrate the themes you discuss.

How should you answer an examination question or write a

coursework essay? The following three-fold structure can help you organise your response:

opening paragraph
developing paragraphs
concluding paragraph.

Opening paragraph. Begin with a paragraph identifying just what topic or issue you will focus on. Show that you have understood what the question is about. You probably will have prepared for particular topics. But look closely at the question and identify key words to see what particular aspect it asks you to write about. Adapt your material to answer that question. Examiners do not reward an essay, however well written, if it is not on the question set.

Developing paragraphs. This is the main body of your essay. In it, you develop your argument, point by point, paragraph by paragraph. Use evidence from the play that illuminates the topic or issue, and answers the question set. Each paragraph makes a point of dramatic or thematic significance. Some paragraphs could make points concerned with context or particular critical approaches. The effect of your argument builds up as each paragraph adds to the persuasive quality of your essay. Use brief quotations that support your argument, and show clearly just why they are relevant. Ensure that your essay demonstrates that you are aware that *Coriolanus* is a play; a drama intended for performance, and therefore open to a wide variety of interpretations and audience responses.

Concluding paragraph. Your final paragraph pulls together your main conclusions. It does not simply repeat what you have written earlier, but summarises concisely how your essay has successfully answered the question.

Example

Question: How does Shakespeare contrst characters to dramatise crucial themes of *Coriolanus*?

The following notes show the 'ingredients' of an answer. In an examination it is usually helpful to prepare similar notes from which you write your essay, paragraph by paragraph. Remember that examiners are not impressed by 'name-dropping': use of critics' names. What they want you to show is your knowledge and judgement of the play and its contexts, and of how it has been interpreted from different critical perspectives.

Opening paragraph

Show you are aware that the question asks you to discuss both character and themes, and to demonstrate the ways in which contrasted characters emphasise key concerns of the play. Because Coriolanus is so dramatically dominant, identify how contrasting him with other characters illustrates those vital preoccupations. So include the following points and aim to write a sentence or more on each:

- Coriolanus is always centre stage in the play. If he is not physically present, other characters talk about him.
- His character embodies certain crucial themes of the play, for example pride, bravery (the Roman virtue, valour), war, patrician rule, mother-love, nobility, ingratitude.
- But all the characters in the play can be seen as dramatic contrasts to Coriolanus. He stands in opposition to each. To contrast Coriolanus with other characters is to show how Shakespeare both illustrates and questions many of the play's central concerns.
- This essay will therefore identify how contrasting Coriolanus with other characters dramatises important themes.

Developing paragraphs

Now write a paragraph or more on major characters showing how their contrast with Coriolanus embodies crucial themes of the play:

- *Volumnia*. Coriolanus' mother both creates and destroys him. She shares his belief in the military values of Rome, but in dramatic contrast with him she is politically skilled. He hates flattery and false appearance, hypocrisy and telling untruths; she is willing to embrace 'policy', or deceitful pretence to achieve her goals. She urges her son to act a part as he begs for votes in the marketplace, and instructs him in the insincere gestures and expressions he can use to persuade the citizens. The contrast illustrates the themes of false appearance and deceit that run through the play. Her willingness to compromise contrasts with his constancy, the theme expressed in her accusation that he is 'too absolute'.

- *Virgilia.* Coriolanus' wife represents the compassionate and tender feelings which Coriolanus lacks. Her 'female' loving values contrast sharply with the militaristic masculinity of Rome: 'O Jupiter, no blood!'
- *The tribunes Sicinius and Brutus.* The thematic contrasts here concern politics and 'service'. Coriolanus' political enemies represent a very different form of State and social justice: democracy versus the autocracy of patrician rule ('What is the city but the people?'). A further contrast is in their notion of 'service' to Rome. Coriolanus sees service as military action, the tribunes see it as political representation of the people.
- *Aufidius.* Coriolanus' rival in war is a contrasting mirror-image of him as a great warrior with whom he has a love–hate relationship. Unlike Coriolanus, Aufidius is a machiavellian figure who plots his downfall. This theme of treachery is also reflected in Coriolanus' switch of allegiance to the Volsces.
- *Cominius.* Coriolanus' fellow soldier is contrasted with him through the different way he treats his troops, and in his measured, formal language. As such he represents a contrasting image of the Roman military hero.
- *The plebeians.* Coriolanus' class enemies, the citizens of Rome, stand in sharp dramatic contrast to the warrior patrician who despises them as inferiors. Their concern is for group action in opposition to his extreme individualism. He loves war and fighting, but they are unwilling soldiers, pressed into military service. He sees them as cowards, more interested in looting than fighting. They also contrast with Coriolanus in constancy (they are fickle, easily swayed by the tribunes).
- *Menenius.* Coriolanus' father-figure contrasts with him in displaying different aspects of Roman patrician behaviour: affability and love of pleasure, pragmatism and willingness to play a part. Menenius talks and tries to flatter his way out of difficult situations. Unlike Coriolanus ('the rock, the oak not to be wind-shaken'), Menenius bends, not breaks; he wishes to 'patch up' Rome's disputes with 'cloth of any colour'.

Concluding paragraph

Write several sentences pulling together your conclusions. You might include the following points:

- All characters, in their contrasts with Coriolanus, deepen the theme of conflict that runs through the play (patricians versus plebeians, Romans versus Volsces, war versus peace, etc.).
- Rome itself can be considered as a 'character' in the play, and its divisions also embody the theme of conflict.
- Coriolanus' own character also displays contrasts which represent the play's themes of divided loyalty, treachery, ingratitude, conflict and change:
  - He is a warrior, son, father, husband, and would-be politician.
  - A successful soldier, he is an unsuccessful politician.
  - A loyal Roman who treacherously defects to the Volsces, he displays the ingratitude he despises in the plebeians.
  - His final submission to his mother shows his vulnerability. He proves false to what he thought was his nature. Love for his mother overrides his desire for revenge.
  - He thus discovers that he cannot be 'alone': free of, or above, society.

Writing about character

Much critical writing about *Coriolanus* traditionally focused on characters, writing about them as if they were living human beings. Today it is not sufficient just to describe their personalities. When you write about characters you will also be expected to show that they are dramatic constructs, part of Shakespeare's stagecraft, instruments of his exploration of politics. They embody the wider concerns of the play, have certain dramatic functions, and are set in a social and political world with particular values and beliefs. They reflect and express issues of significance to Shakespeare's society – and today's.

Of course you should say what a character seems like to you, but you should also write about how Shakespeare makes him or her part of his overall dramatic design. But there is a danger in writing about the functions of characters or the character types they represent. To reduce a character to a mere plot device is just as inappropriate as treating him or her as a real person.

When you write about characters in *Coriolanus* you should therefore try to achieve a balance between analysing their personality, identifying the dilemmas they face, and placing them in their social, critical and dramatic contexts. That style of writing is found all through this Guide, and that, together with the essay example given above (pages 120–3) and the following brief discussions of Coriolanus and Volumnia, can help your own written responses.

Coriolanus

Coriolanus' name, Martius, gives an initial clue to his character (Mars is the Roman god of war). He embodies 'valour', the prime virtue of the Roman patricians, and possesses *gressus*, a swaggering air of superiority. But there is no single key to Coriolanus' character. Right at the start of the play the First Citizen identifies four sources of his brave deeds: desire for fame, love of Rome, the wish to please his mother, and pride (Act 1 Scene 1, lines 27–30). Much later in the play, Aufidius locates three flaws in Coriolanus' character: 'pride', 'defect of judgement' and his inflexible 'nature' which made him act in peace-time exactly as he had acted in war (Act 4 Scene 7, lines 37–45).

Coriolanus is contemptuous of the plebeians, always ready to revile them. He is choleric and impatient, unable to control his temper and emotionally immature, exploding at key moments in knee-jerk responses to anything that touches his sense of honour. He values his nobility, and seeks honour in war, yet is offended by praise, and disdainful of material reward for his military exploits. Successful in war, he fails utterly in peace. He cries 'I banish you', when the reality is that the people of Rome banish him. He joins the Volsces and seeks to destroy Rome. Coriolanus thinks he can survive and succeed 'alone', but family bonds prove too strong, and love for his mother overcomes his desire for revenge. He finally gives in to his mother's plea, spares Rome, and thus signs his own death warrant at the hands of Aufidius and his Volsces.

Volumnia

Coriolanus' mother has brought him up with a taboo on tenderness: every human feeling must be suppressed other than the joy of serving Rome in war. Volumnia devotes her life to turning her son into a fighting machine ('To a cruel war I sent him'), rejoicing in his wounds and the honour they bring. She plans for Coriolanus to become

Consul, the most important political person in Rome. In the patriarchal society of Rome, women lack power, but Volumnia burns with ambition to place her son in the position of greatest authority.

Volumnia has been described as ruthless and calculating, a politically skilled schemer obsessed with bloodshed and wars. She knows how to manipulate her son through his pride, his sense of honour, and his feelings for her. She uses psychological blackmail on him to achieve her purposes. But, at the end of the play, her pleading for Rome proves fatal for her son.

Political groups in Rome

Coriolanus' Rome was neither a monarchy nor a democracy, but a republic ruled by an aristocracy, the patricians. Some brief definitions are given below, and you will find further help with the political structure of Rome throughout the play (especially pages 5, 22–4, 41–2 and 103–4).

- *Patricians.* The ruling elite; wealthy aristocrats; the law-makers.
- *Plebeians.* Citizens and workers; neither patricians nor slaves.
- *Tribunes.* Spokesmen of the plebeians, defenders of their rights.
- *Aediles.* Officers of the tribunes, carrying out their orders.
- *The Senate.* The law-making body of Rome; the seat of government.
- *Senators.* Patricians who sat in the Senate.
- *The Capitol.* The meeting house of the Senate.
- *Consul.* Each year the Senate nominated two Consuls, to serve jointly for one year only, as commanders in chief of the army and heads of state. The plebeians were expected to ratify the appointment in a show of general assent. Their rejection of Coriolanus as Consul leads to his banishment.

Resources

Books

Janet Adelman, *Suffocating Mothers: Fantasies of Maternal Origin in Shakespeare's Plays, Hamlet to The Tempest*, Routledge 1992

Using a psychoanalytic approach, Adelman identifies eating as the central image of the play, with Volumnia as the non-nourishing mother, the crowd as an infantile common mouth, and Coriolanus' attitude to the plebeians' voices and his abhorrence of praise expressed in language which 'depends on his attitude toward food'. Adelman's essay is also reprinted as 'Escaping the Matrix: The Construction of Masculinity in *Coriolanus*', in Susan Zimmerman (ed.), *Shakespeare's Tragedies: Contemporary Critical Essays*, Macmillan 1998

A C Bradley, 'Character and the imaginative appeal of tragedy in *Coriolanus*', in B A Brockman (ed.), *Shakespeare: Coriolanus, A Casebook*, Macmillan 1977

An approach to the play mainly through character. Argues that in Coriolanus' 'huge violent heart there was a store, not only of tender affection, but of delicate and chivalrous poetry'.

B A Brockman (ed.), *Shakespeare: Coriolanus, A Casebook*, Macmillan 1977

Contains a valuable collection of critical writing on *Coriolanus* from 1765 to 1971 including criticism by Bradley, Burke, Charney, Knights, Rossiter and Traversi noted in this booklist.

Kenneth Burke, 'The Delights of Faction', in B A Brockman (ed.), *Shakespeare: Coriolanus, A Casebook*, Macmillan 1977

Considers Coriolanus as a scapegoat, whose symbolic sacrifice affords audience pleasure.

Maurice Charney, *Shakespeare's Roman Plays: The Function of Imagery in the Drama*, Harvard University Press 1961

A much more thorough-going examination of the imagery of *Coriolanus* than those of Clemen and Spurgeon, and especially alert to the dramatic function of images. An extract is printed in B A Brockman (ed.), *Shakespeare: Coriolanus, A Casebook*, Macmillan 1977

W H Clemen, *The Development of Shakespeare's Imagery*, Methuen 1951

The chapter on *Coriolanus* claims that the dominant imagery of the play arises from the plebeian–patrician conflict: images of disdain and disgust for 'the rabble', contrasting with those that express 'the heroic nature of Coriolanus'.

Terry Eagleton, *William Shakespeare*, Basil Blackwell 1986

Although Eagleton includes only a short section on *Coriolanus* (comparing *Coriolanus* with *Hamlet*), his book exemplifies postmodern (or deconstructive) approaches to Shakespeare's plays.

D J Enright, 'Coriolanus: Tragedy or Debate?', *Essays in Criticism*, iv 1954
An early 'political' approach, arguing that Rome's factions diminish human potential.

Harley Granville-Barker, *Prefaces to Shakespeare: Coriolanus*, Nick Hern Books 1993
A detailed scene-by-scene commentary and discussion of characters, verse, act-division and stage directions. Asserts that *Coriolanus* lacks the 'transcendent vitality and metaphysical power' of Shakespeare's great tragedies.

Coppelia Kahn, *Roman Shakespeare: Warriors, Wounds, and Women*, Taylor and Francis 1996
A feminist study that explores the gender ideologies behind 'Roman virtue'. Argues that as the play moves from battlefield to politics it 'begins to reveal the self-cancelling nature of a masculinity that is maternally authorised'.

Victor Kiernan, *Eight Tragedies of Shakespeare: A Marxist Study*, Verso 1996
Argues that Shakespeare's personal experience is expressed in his plays as sympathy for the poor. For Kiernan, *Coriolanus* is in many ways 'a study of aristocratic flattery and cajoling of the people for the purpose of duping them'.

Bruce King, *Coriolanus*, Macmillan 1989
A lively introduction to the variety of criticism, fully aware of the limitations of each. King wryly concludes 'the critical methods we employ are themselves sources of distortion while being necessary. That's life in the postmodern age.'

G Wilson Knight, *The Imperial Theme*, Taylor and Francis 1965
Shakespeare's Roman plays are interpreted through cosmic images, symbolism and themes. Knight's vigorous and imaginative readings are today regarded as controversial, but his discussion of *Coriolanus* is still well worth reading.

L C Knights, 'Shakespeare and Political Wisdom: The Personalism of Julius Caesar and Coriolanus', in B A Brockman (ed.), *Shakespeare: Coriolanus, A Casebook*, Macmillan 1977
Argues that 'Coriolanus' tragedy is that he cannot grow up', and that the play superbly demonstrates 'that disruption in the state – the body politic – is related to individual disharmony . . . public crisis is rooted in the personal and habitual'.

Jan Kott, *Shakespeare Our Contemporary*, Methuen 1965
An influential but now much criticised political reading of Shakespeare's plays. Kott's chapter on *Coriolanus* claims 'Coriolanus wants to destroy the world, because the world contradicts the laws of nature. But in the name of the same laws of nature Coriolanus has been condemned by his mother, wife and son.'

Wyndham Lewis, *The Lion and the Fox: The Role of the Hero in the Plays of Shakespeare*, Methuen 1966
Argues that Coriolanus does not grow up, and is 'a conventional military hero, existing as the characteristic ornament of a strong aristocratic society'.

Adrian Poole, *Coriolanus*, Harvester Wheatsheaf 1988

A valuable critical study which identifies how characters constantly project images of their own emotions and beliefs onto Coriolanus. Works carefully through the play, always alert to how language creates dramatic effect.

A P Rossiter, *Angel with Horns*, Longman 1961

Judges *Coriolanus* to be Shakespeare's 'only great political play' and claims that, like the history plays, it is about power and the State. An extract is printed in B A Brockman (ed.), *Shakespeare: Coriolanus, A Casebook*, Macmillan 1977

Caroline Spurgeon, *Shakespeare's Imagery and What It Tells Us*, Cambridge University Press 1935

The first major study of imagery in the plays. Although much criticised today, Spurgeon's identification of image-clusters as a dominant feature of the plays has influenced later studies. Claims that the dominant imagery of *Coriolanus* arises from the theme of the body and sickness.

Derek A Traversi, 'The World of Coriolanus', in B A Brockman (ed.), *Shakespeare: Coriolanus, A Casebook*, Macmillan 1977

Argues that 'the key to Coriolanus's tragedy' lies in great part in 'the isolation from his fellow men which birth and prejudice have combined to impose upon him'.

Films

1984 *Coriolanus* Director: Elijah Moshinsky, Coriolanus: Alan Howard

Made for the BBC/Time-Life series. Set and costumes are Jacobean, but the battle scenes use Ancient Greek helmets and shields. The text is quite heavily cut, but Alan Howard's brass-lunged delivery catches Coriolanus' contempt and pride.

A loosely adapted version of *Coriolanus* was made in Italy in 1964, *Coriolano, eroe senza patria* (Coriolanus, hero without a country). It was marketed internationally as *Thunder of Battle*.

Audio books

Versions are available in the series by Naxos, Arkangel, Harper Collins and the BBC Radio Collection.

Coriolanus on the Web

If you type 'Coriolanus Shakespeare' into your search engine, it may find over 17,000 items. Because websites are of wildly varying quality, and rapidly disappear or are created, no recommendation can safely be made. But if you have time to browse, you may find much of interest.